PRAISE
SACRED GEOMETRY

Sacred Geometry is like a text from an ancient mystery school written for modernity. The teachings are rich, insightful and perhaps most importantly, essential to our spiritual lives. The book is fabulous.

— Caroline Myss, author of *Anatomy of the Spirit* and *Sacred Contracts*

A masterpiece! I've known the authors for years and have impatiently waited for their book. It's here and it's stunning. Just reading it can increase your awareness, consciousness, and inner power. I love it!

— Dr. Joe Vitale, author, *Zero Limits* and *The Miracle.*

The wisdom found in this beautiful book is both profoundly spiritual and extremely practical. I love how the magnificent Gail and Gregory show us the universal picture of how we can embody the power of the divine archetypes of creation and at the same time ground it in science. I believe this is an essential handbook for those who want to live an inspired and awakened life.

— Debra Poneman, bestselling author and founder
Yes to Success and Ageless Seminars

"Gail Hoag and Gregory Hoag are renowned innovators in the field of sacred geometry. Their book *Sacred Geometry: The Universal Language of Divine Alignment* is a powerful text demonstrating their understanding and knowledge of this field.

Their focus on consciousness is one of the most important aspects of this book, and is a topic they brilliantly explore. The Hoags demonstrate how sacred geometry can be used to accelerate consciousness and how precise shapes can manifest vibrationally for significant and positive changes for the harmony of our health and life. *Sacred Geometry* is a worthy contribution to anyone's library."

— Andi Goldman & Jonathan Goldman, Authors
***The Humming Effect* and**
Chakra Frequency

Gregory and Gail Hoag have created the most comprehensive view of Sacred Geometry in our time. Harkening back to the works of John Michell and Robert Lawlor, Greg and Gail have given us the gift of understanding the Divine language of the Universe.

Sacred Geometry: The Universal Language of Divine Alignment is the book we have been waiting for a long time. This is a great gift to anyone who wonders what Sacred Geometry is and why it is so important to our being.

— Jay Weidner Author of *Mysteries of the Great Cross at Hendaye: Alchemy and the End of Time*

We live in a complex world, one that most people struggle to understand, as there is little awareness of the forces - mostly unseen - that mold our life experiences. Gregory and Gail have carefully, clearly and logically explained the workings of this greater reality.

This book is so easy to read, it draws you in from the very beginning, explaining the interconnectedness, the Oneness behind all things. This book will open the eyes of many!

— Prageet Harris, The Stargate Experience

Sacred Geometry: The Universal Language of Divine Alignment by Gregory and Gail Hoag explores the higher dimensional realms of geometry within ourselves, our surroundings, and the universe. In doing so, it enables us to accelerate our awakening, and paths to higher levels of consciousness. I highly recommend this book to everyone for personal and spiritual growth.

— Fred Grover Jr. M.D. Integrative Medicine Physician and author of *Spiritual Genomics and Awakening Gaia*

Stunning in its revelations *Sacred Geometry: The Universal Language of Divine Alignment* is a breathtaking shift into higher consciousness as you experience an amazing understanding of the genius codes of divine form, pattern and number at the core of each one of us.

Divinely inspired and grounded by a lifetime of synchronicity and research, Gregory and Gail Hoag whisk you away on an adventure into the deepest spiritual knowledge, a cosmic story made earthbound.

This is essential wisdom for anyone desiring to live masterfully at this time of a great quantum shift in a truer understanding of life and our connection to one another and divine source, prophesied by the great wisdom traditions.

— Dianne Collins, Creator of Quantum Think®,
Author of *Do You QuantumThink? New Thinking That Will Rock Your World*

If you are curious about what is *Sacred Geometry*, how does it work and how can it help you gain clarity and guide you in the challenging, uncertain times we are witnessing today, this masterpiece of research, deep knowledge and personal experience will give you a valuable perspective on the patterns of creation and how you can use this Divine Wisdom to enjoy and relax on your magical journey of life.

— Alan K. Collins,
Master QuantumThink® Coach

Sacred Geometry: The Universal Language of Divine Alignment by Gregory and Gail Hoag guides readers on a transformative journey toward expanded consciousness. The book intricately intertwines science, mathematics, logic and reason with spirituality, inviting readers to explore the profound and perfect interconnectedness of our existence in the earth realm with all of nature and creation.

Gregory and Gail make the esoteric concepts of sacred geometry accessible to a diverse audience, satisfying the rational mind and engaging the soul's quest for deeper understanding. *Sacred Geometry: The Universal Language of Divine Alignment* is an enlightening and powerful tool for personal self-discovery, guiding readers toward a richer understanding of their role as co-creators with the Universe.

— Waxéla Sananda,
Shaman, trainer and
podcast host

Sacred Geometry: The Universal Language of Divine Alignment by Gail and Gregory Hoag is a captivating journey into the world of sacred geometry, going beyond its visual beauty to uncover the deep connections and harmonious patterns that define the universe. In a world facing seemingly insurmountable challenges, the wisdom within sacred geometry provides practical solutions for healing and growth. The book's clear, engaging narrative and beautiful illustrations make it accessible and appealing to a wide audience, making it a must-read for those interested in spirituality, metaphysics, and the potential for positive change in our world.

— Mark Porteous,
Soul Affiliate Alliance Co-founder

Greg and Gail are masters of multi-dimensional alchemy. Their book is an energetic awakening— a progressive journey through the wisdom of sacred geometry, with so many 'ah hahs' along the way. You'll have new eyes to see the intrinsic majesty of our Universe.

— Jonette Crowley, spiritual teacher,
author, channel

I met Gregory about 40 years ago and he has never stopped investigating the nature of reality and the universe. This book with his partner Gail is the culmination of a lifetime work and deep diving into the realms of creation that have set it apart from all those that have followed in the footsteps of the Hoags. It is a beaming beautiful book. Buy it now.

— Alan Steinfeld, Host of NewRealities,
Author of *Making Contact*

This book masterfully guides us to greater understanding of the unseen and unknown so that we may tap into the fullness of our human experience and our potential. The authors have taken complex subject matters in science, spirituality and nature and through their in-depth explanations and illustrations have given us a blueprint for our own lives.

— Nancy Matthews, International
Speaker, Author

As I read *Sacred Geometry: The Universal Language of Divine Alignment*, I felt the effect of the higher dimensional wisdom pouring through Gail and Gregory into me. Their light and connection are profound. If you wish to speed up your awakening and ascension, please do read this book!

— Rev. Lisa Barnett, Founder of Akashic Knowing School of Wisdom & Author of 4 Akashic Books

Sacred Geometry

THE UNIVERSAL LANGUAGE OF DIVINE ALIGNMENT

GREGORY HOAG
GAIL HOAG

Published by
Hybrid Global Publishing
333 E 14th Street
#3C
New York, NY 10003

Manufactured in the United States of America, or in the United Kingdom when distributed elsewhere.

Hoag, Gregory.
Hoag, Gail.
Sacred Geometry
ISBN: 978-1-961757-35-6
eBook: 978-1-961757-36-3
LCCN: 2024901168

Cover design by: Julia Kuris
Copyediting by: Wendie Pecharsky
Interior design by: Suba Murugan
Author photo by: Rebecca Ryan
Photos of Metaforms and land by: Gregory Hoag
Illustrations by: Gregory Hoag and Gail Hoag with purchases images from Deposit Books and Shutterstock

Website: https://iconnect2all.com/
Email: office@iconnect2all.com

CONTENTS

ACKNOWLEDGMENTS

Over the last 40 years, we've had many people whose influence, knowledge and friendship have played an important role in supporting our work and we wish to acknowledge some of those people here.

The seed of Metaforms was sparked by Dr. Frank Alper in 1981 and his support continued on for many years. We deeply appreciate Frank's teaching, books, friendship and his role in performing our marriage ceremony in 1985.

Early on with our work, we were blessed to meet and learn from some of the giants of Sacred Geometry knowledge: Keith Critchlow, John Michell, Robert Lawlor, Michael S. Schneider and J. J. Hurtak. Some other people that influenced our work are Jonathan Goldman, Drunvalo Melchizedek, Graham Hancock, Randall Carlson and David Wilcock.

We want to thank and acknowledge the wonderful support and friendship over the years that we received from our dearest friends, Marian and Glenn Head, who have played a loving, joyful and amazing role in our lives for so many years. Many friends and colleagues have been there for us including Bob Gulick, David Tresemer, Prageet Harris, John Yukas, Bob Wood, GW Hardin, John Abell, Alayna McKee and Scott Smith.

The business of bringing Metaforms to the world has been lovingly supported by the work of Lee and Tammy Erickson, Mark Porteous, Sean Allen, Edgard Chillin, Caitlin Watson, Mike Seiler and Steve Sky. We appreciate the focus, detail and high quality energy they have all brought.

Writing a book is a huge task and we greatly appreciate the contributions of our publisher Karen Strauss and editor Claudia Volkman to make this book a reality.

We are grateful for the amazing people we have not named who have recognized the importance of our work, products and taught us a great deal from their experiences. There have been many wonderful friends whose love and support have been very important to us, as well as our dear children and family that we love so dearly.

In addition, we deeply value the influence of wonderful masters, guides and teachers that have been a part of our journey. Many of these beings have worked with us from higher dimensions and their guidance, encouragement and clarity has been steadfast.

INTRODUCTION

GAIL'S STORY

Meeting Gregory was a pivotal event in what had already been an extraordinary life path. At age three, I had an epiphany that led me to become conscious that my purpose was to be a catalyst for positive transformation. I was outside swinging on my swing set when I experienced an enlightening moment that jolted me with this powerful awareness. Honestly, I didn't know where it came from or what triggered it. I remember that my heart was wildly expanded, and I was filled with enthusiasm. I ran into the house to find my mother and explain what had happened and that I wanted my middle name to be "Joy." Her response was bland, something like, "Oh, that's nice dear." She didn't get the enormity of what had happened to me, and I realized right then and there that this inner truth was mine to follow and to search out what it meant. (I took that middle name of "Joy" when Gregory and I married 32 years later.)

As a young child, I was a stargazer and developed an evening ritual of connecting with the celestial night sky. I believe this is how I taught myself to meditate, unbeknownst to me. As I felt connected with the stars beyond, I filled myself with wonder and love, aligning with where I belonged. Sometimes, this generated out-of-body experiences, which felt light, airy, and pretty freaky to me. Without support for this level of sensitivity I felt like a stranger and wondered how I got to where I was and why. Surely, I had been dropped off at the wrong address!

I tell you this not to say I'm different—quite the contrary. I believe each of us has had strong connections when our intuition, creativity, and wonder were intact. These were the times the soul was directing us before the demands of dominant family, socio-cultural, and religious imprinting took hold. It is fundamental that we remember who we truly are and reclaim the connections that support the expression of soul in this lifetime. Putting the clues back together brings clarity to our purpose and addresses some of the deep schisms we feel.

Receiving inspiration and recognizing intuitive abilities is quite wonderful, but often, it does not come with specific instructions. Our education and social norms don't prepare us to develop and use the creative/feminine parts of our consciousness. As a teenager, I became increasingly aware of my need to write poetry, journal, and tap into my artistic nature. Since I had very little instruction or encouragement, I kept these feelings deeply private, locked inside.

This driving force became integrated into my life as I left for college and unearthed the passions I couldn't pursue in suburban Baltimore. It was the late 1960s, and I came face to face with new attitudes of freedom and friends who encouraged me to live with purpose and reach outside the norms I grew up with. It was an enormous time of experimentation and I challenged many of the beliefs I was raised to accept. The courage and determination I found marked me deeply and placed me on a circuitous path that made it clear I would be part of pioneering something new and different. At that time, I had lots of questions about social values and realized I hadn't reached maturity for providing answers.

In my 20s, I saw a world in great need of wisdom and higher values, which attracted me to become a political activist. But after several years of organizing, lobbying, protesting, and advocating, which often ended in frustration, everything seemed to fall apart. I realized that things don't change on the outside without foundational shifts. It is the inside or inner world that is the crucial place to work.

Shortly afterward, something very potent happened to me. I fell ill with what was diagnosed as pelvic inflammatory disease, and my doctor recommended hospitalization. Before he checked me into the hospital, he said something like, "Don't worry. We'll take care of you now, and you can just relax." Something went off in my head and I developed the expectation that others were taking care of me; I let go of my inner responsibility and determination for my well-being. I didn't even fathom what I was doing and just how ill I was. The nurses hooked me up to massive intravenous doses of antibiotics, but within a few days, the infection worsened with a fever that was dangerously on the rise. The drugs weren't working, and I was unresponsive to the treatment. I was definitely going in the wrong direction, and my energy and mental clarity were falling apart. Yet, I was still feeling loyal to my doctors and thought they would take care of this situation, unaware of how close I was heading to the edge of life.

At this point, my fever spiked so high that it caused a state of delirium. I realized something very strange was happening. I was in a tunnel of light and in the process of leaving my body. I was totally calm and held an inner state of acceptance and peace. It was actually a beautiful, highly connected experience. That's when I heard the voice that really got my attention! "You are leaving this life if you continue, and you have a choice." Whoa. That moment put me back in touch with something very significant. I wasn't ready to go yet. I felt I had a life of purpose ahead of me, and I certainly hadn't accomplished that much yet! It was at that edge of life when I engaged my soul, and with all the energy, will, and determination I had ever known, I literally pulled myself back into my body. Shortly thereafter, my high fever started to decline, and the healing process slowly took hold. That experience changed me massively. The reconnection with soul and higher purpose was profound. As soon as I took responsibility for my life and committed to living my life with purpose, the vital life force energy returned, and I began to heal. This near-death experience eliminated any fear of death I may have held previously and left me with a feeling of divine acceptance. Life was truly about the Soul, and this set me on a mission to understand the play of higher knowledge and spiritual guidance. I deeply valued my intuition and the ability to hear the messages that could direct my life choices. I also crafted a very different attitude about health and the medical establishment, realizing that putting my life in someone else's hands is dead wrong. I embarked on a journey to better understand health, the healing arts, and my spiritual connections.

In the following years, I was no longer satisfied playing the game of life I'd been taught and engaged in self-reflection, as well as an exploration of my creativity through art. I found a mentor who opened me up to my artistic gifts, and I spent hours upon hours in museums studying the master artists' deep and intricate interpretations of our physical world. I loved finding a way to express the insights and passions I had been feeling for so long. I felt passionately alive as meaningful connections were growing. I learned once again to empty my mind, move beyond the internal chatter, and allow myself to be directed through intuition and Soul connection. I explored light, color, and movement to build visual platforms—paintings—for the viewer to contemplate and explore their inner world.

During this time, I discovered the work of R. Buckminster Fuller and his amazing geometric gestalt. He led me on a journey to understand Universe from the perspective of geometry. I loved following his tangents of expanded awareness to explain the physical world. He also brought me to a deeper understanding of "integrity" and was one among others who shaped my cosmology. I devoured his books. I was fortunate to attend one of his lectures in Washington, D.C., at the National Academy of Science. He took me on an inner and outer journey, touching my heart with his love of Universe.

I spent a couple of years in New York City, barely surviving as a struggling artist, taking on temporary positions as a commercial artist. I call this period my Dark Night of the Soul as I was rebounding from a painful divorce and trying to find myself once again. Along with creating some powerful new paintings, I took some workshops to get back in touch with my inner self. I had some astounding meditative experiences that urged me to remember that my life was meant for much more. I began to journal again, and at the end of many of the messages, I wrote, "Go to the Mountain." I thought this was merely a metaphor until I was invited to visit Colorado, a part of the country I had never considered. Within a few days of being in Boulder, Colorado, I was inundated with messages and a voice within telling me to leave New York and move to the mountains. It made no sense; however, the voice only became clearer. Within a month, in January of 1984, I had moved into a magical hobbit house in Boulder and, among other things, was cultivating my spiritual ability to connect with higher intelligence and channel information.

My dear friend Glenn Head invited me to attend a transformational workshop called *Money and You*, taught by Marshall Thurber. It was another pivotal experience, and I was delighted that Bucky Fuller had been a mentor to Marshall. Fuller's wisdom came through many of the core beliefs of this program, and I was once again reunited with his magnificent spirit.

Although Bucky Fuller passed on in 1983, I believed that his consciousness was still available, and I asked if I could continue to learn from him. Several weeks later, while in meditation, I made contact with his soul and became an honored student of his teachings. I wrote down as many of these transmissions as I could; however, after a number of sessions, I realized the detail and science I was receiving were beyond what I could make use of. Being a practical person, I asked him to either curtail these lessons or help connect me with someone I could collaborate with. Quite soon after, I met Gregory, who was carrying a box of Sacred Geometry sculptures he had welded. I asked him if he was aware of Bucky Fuller's work, and he told me he had no knowledge of him. I felt it was important to introduce Gregory to Bucky's universal understanding and invited him to a channeling I was giving in a few days. It was this event that initiated our relationship and the recognition that we had a common mission. Within weeks, it was apparent that we had work to do together. I suspected that Bucky had a hand in this matchmaking.

Five months after meeting, we married in 1985 and began our work together. It was serendipitous that Universe brought us together just as Gregory's previous business of ten years was winding down. We worked with higher spiritual principles to complete unfinished business, relationships, and personal issues to clear the path for our future together. It was a powerful blend of consciousness, art, science, and business knowledge. We recognized that our partnership was a unique and critical aspect of effectively living our purpose.

We were both walking a spiritual path that begged us to bring our metaphysical knowledge into the physical world. I had been receiving intuitive guidance that taught me how to work with healing energies, so I was extremely sensitive to the Sacred Geometries that Gregory was making. Together, we realized that we were at the center of developing a technology that would be quite relevant and valuable in the evolution of consciousness and health. We were inundated with blessings of serendipity that connected us with teachings and influential people and directed us to the knowledge and connections we needed at each step. This supported our personal growth and the creation of Metaforms' energetic technologies and transformative tools.

For over 38 years, we have been learning, growing, teaching, and creating Sacred Geometry technologies that have landed in most countries around the world and connected us to tens of thousands of people. We've learned from our higher curiosity, extraordinary connection to guidance, a network of friends, hard work, mistakes, and down-to-earth miracles. We continue this journey compelled by our souls that recognize the importance of this time of transition and both of us are filled with deep gratitude and love for this opportunity to play and serve.

GREGORY'S STORY

Before my birth, I worked with my mother for years to get the timing right. From my higher, soul perspective, I could understand the divine patterns of the stars and planets coming together on October 4, 1947, at a precise time to optimally support me in the creativity needed for my life path. A chart composed of Libra, Leo, and Scorpio with no oppositions, no squares, and no Earth. I've been able to access those memories, explore past lives, and receive information from beings of higher dimensional realms, but that has not always been so.

As a child, I didn't understand my birth choice because my earth experience followed one of the agreements we all share: each of us moving through the birth canal forgets everything before our first breath as the soul enters the body. So, with no memory of what came before, how did I gain these new beliefs? The answer is a catalyst so significant that it has transformed everything in my reality and given me the presence of living life from a soul perspective.

Is there anything more powerful than this thing called belief? Beliefs drive us forward or paralyze us completely. Everything is conditioned by our beliefs, from the way we see and interact with our world to the way it interacts with us. As we look closer, do any of our beliefs really originate with us out of personal experience? Very few come from within us; most are gifts from family, teachers, and friends handed down from one generation to another and from one reality to another. We develop a pattern of accepting other's realities as our own.

Sometimes, we do things just because everyone else does. I'm reminded of how the phrase "knock on wood" came about. Over two-thousand years ago, druids, an ancient priesthood, existed in England. Trees were sacred to them and were believed to be inhabited by high vibrational spirits or devas. When a druid was about to begin a journey, he would enter a sacred grove of oak trees, knock upon one to awaken the spirit within, and ask for good fortune for his travels. Today, thousands of years later, people are still rapping on a metal desk with a wood-grain vinyl veneer for good luck.

During college in the 1960s, I spent the first few years studying the sciences and writing a paper against the existence of God, but in my final years, I opened up to literature and the arts. Upon graduating in 1970, I stepped onto a new path as I was beginning to realize I was trapped in what spiritual masters call an illusion. For ten years, I explored different Eastern masters, receiving numerous initiations, meditations, and residences in several ashrams. I was searching for the experience that would take me beyond all beliefs and then melt into the background like an enigmatic riddle with no clear answer.

In 1980, when I was 32, it happened; kundalini started flowing through my body, awakening me to the higher realms of my being. *Kundalini* is a Sanskrit term for the energy that is coiled at the base of the spine and, when awakened, flows upward through all the chakras, connecting the physical body to the higher realms of energy and consciousness. Gopi Krishna, a yogi, mystic, and teacher born in Kashmir, India, experienced the awakening of the spiritual force known as kundalini in 1937 at the age of 34. The understanding of kundalini is steeped in the spiritual lore of the Indian subcontinent, one of the more spiritually oriented parts of the world. However, when Gopi Krishna had his awakening, he was unable to find another teacher or master anywhere who could counsel him on his ordeal from a place of experience and help him navigate the life-threatening flow of energy transforming his consciousness and physical body. Through his dedicated work and exploration, he wrote books about this phenomenon with the intent of expanding scientific understanding of the higher dimensions and how they are part of the spiritual cycle of growth for all human beings.

> **This mechanism, known as kundalini, is the real cause of all genuine spiritual and psychic phenomena;**

> the biological basis of evolution and development of personality; the secret origin of all esoteric and occult doctrines; the master key to the unsolved mystery of creation; the inexhaustible source of philosophy, art, and science; and the fountainhead of all religious faiths, past, present, and future.[1]
>
> The evolution of human beings, in actual fact, signifies the evolution of their consciousness, of the vital principle inhabiting the body, by which alone the embodied self can become cognizant of its true immortal state. It does not signify merely the development of the intellect or reason, which are but instruments of the indwelling spirit, but of the whole personality, of both its conscious and subconscious parts, which involves an overhauling and reshaping of the organic machine to make it a fit abode for a higher intelligence, essentially superior in nature to that which resides in the normal human body.[2]

Gopi Krishna struggled in pain and endured life-threatening situations with his body for years. This energy can kill you or drive you insane, and that is what the spiritual masters that he consulted were telling him, but none of them had a direct experience, so consequently, their support was confusing and ineffectual.

What catalyzed my experience of kundalini rising was a pyramid that I had built with a friend. I was living with him, his

---

1 Gopi Krishna, Living with Kundalini (Boston: Shambhala Publications, Inc., 1993), 257.

2 Living with Kundalini, 185.

wife, and two children after moving out of an ashram. We were flying to California for personal sessions with Kevin Ryerson, a channeler made famous by Shirley MacLaine, and over a number of sessions, Kevin channeled the plans for a geometrical structure that, although it was only eight feet high, cost us more than $50,000 to build. In today's dollars, which would be more than $200,000.

Despite just moving out of my second ashram experience, I had the money. Yes, I was told that I needed to renounce worldly possessions when I entered, but the challenge was that I owned the building the ashram was in as well as many of their vehicles, and I employed most of the people in the ashram. My business had over twenty-five employees and was selling $500,000 worth of belt buckles a year. Mahatmas (spiritual directors of the guru) were trying to figure out how to deal with me and maintain the ashram. I was now arguing as much *for* spirituality as I used to argue *against* it when I was in college, but still the problem was I didn't fit into their box of how it was supposed to work. They couldn't figure it out, so they closed the ashram and left the messy details of resolving the finances with all of the residents to me. I just took it as a scene change and dove into the pyramid project with my friend.

The angles were modeled after the main pyramid on the Giza Plateau in Egypt, and it was constructed of thick stainless-steel tubing with precise connectors and angles designed by engineers from the University of Colorado. We filled the tubing with crushed quartz and had a three-foot-high crystal at the base with a parabolic reflector beneath it. The crystal had all seven of its chakras intact. Above it was a two-foot diameter crystal ball that took a year to cut in a German facility. We had three more large crystal balls aligned in the capstone, which was made out of thick layers of gold over silver over copper. A hand-dyed silk cloth enclosed the entire structure.

When the pyramid was completed, we began trading off nights sleeping in it for a period of several weeks. What happened for me was unique: My Soul took this as an opportunity to awaken my kundalini. Although awakening to a higher self sounds wonderful, and it was what I was seeking, my experience was quite the opposite. To begin, I had no idea what was happening to me. Energy was shooting up my spine like a geyser, and when it hit my throat chakra, where it encountered resistance to the level of openness needed to share greater truths, it exploded. Certainly, I had issues, and this was like cleaning house with a fire hose: It looked much worse before it got better. My nervous system was a 110V circuit trying to run 220V. It burned like a cold fire and was literally burning holes in my feet and hands as the energy tried to move through my body, meeting resistance in its passage. The chakra points in the middle of each hand and foot were blistering. As soon as one blister broke, another began. My flesh was disappearing as slow holes were working their way through my extremities. I thought all this higher energy stuff was supposed to be subtle, but there was very little that felt subtle about this energy flow, which was transforming my physical body to become a receiver of higher vibrational energy flow.

At times I was sailing through the Universe and communicating with beings in other dimensions. I was vividly reliving past lives involving my friend and his wife, and believe me, it is a blessing to deal with the awareness of only one life at a time. As the remembering of past lives continued, it made it very difficult to know whom I was relating to and how to relate. In the little bits of lucid thought that I could muster, I remember thinking that this is what it must be like to be schizophrenic. My personality had melted, and I had no GPS in time and space to locate myself. After months of drama, I slowly began to reintegrate with my life in Boulder, Colorado, and my business, which is where I ended up sleeping because no one else wanted me around. No one could make any sense of what I was going through and what I was becoming. Ironically, neither did I, but I knew I could never go back to the old worldview I once had.

A year after my kundalini awakening, I still did not know what had happened to me. I was walking to the home of a healer, David, who had agreed to help me, and I heard a voice say, "This is kundalini." I shared that with David as I walked through his door. He agreed. By that time, I had started welding bronze geometric forms that I was seeing on the higher levels, archetypal energies that existed before physical matter was draped on them. David was having me use the kundalini energy to integrate both sides of my brain and then spin the forms I was building in my mind's eye and listen to the tones they were making. Next, he asked me to ground these energies into my solar plexus. His cat was sitting on my lap at the time I moved the energy down, and as I did so the cat yowled and jumped eight feet out of the room. David looked at me and said, "Well, I guess you did it."

This was about the time when the energy was burning holes in my feet and hands. When a healer moved crystals in circles near my third eye, the flesh would physically move to follow them. I had never felt my forehead muscles move in circles, so I was alternately mesmerized and freaked out. The energies seemed to be increasing, and the different healers that I consulted told me that they would be unable to quiet or reverse the flow if it continued in this manner. I had to take responsibility for what was being created and ground the energy running through my physical and higher bodies. I simplified my diet, avoided spices, and started eating more root vegetables. I went barefoot on the earth, grew plants, and dug in the earth with my hands. I worked to release the blockages and fears within my body as Mother Kundalini brought them into my awareness. I avoided drugs, alcohol, sex, and crowds—all stimulants. I became very empathic, feeling other's energies and emotions, and found it necessary to shut down and block my crown chakra and third eye, reopening them only to receive what was absolutely necessary. I stopped meditating to reduce raising the energy by focusing on my crown chakra, dampening my upper chakras to soften the tide of kundalini, and in doing so, I discovered that I had been energetically intertwined with some of the gurus that I had worked with in the past. Some did not allow a clear, direct connection with Source. They would draw off some of the energy as a toll, so to speak. This was an important discovery as one of the impediments to my connection to the Oneness within me. Each of us is worthy of a direct connection with Source each step of the way.

Recently, I came across a Tibetan thangka painting, which is a sacred image of a deity that is precisely drawn reflecting the energetic aspects of that deity. This was a painting of the White Tara, and she is the only deity to have an eye in the center of each hand and each foot as well as a third eye in the middle of her forehead.

In Hinduism, the White Tara is a form of the female primordial energy known as shakti, which in its highest expression is kundalini. In the literature, they say her extra eyes represent her omniscience, and she is always shown sitting in meditation with her feet upward toward the heavens, with one hand offering blessing and the other offering support. While gazing upon her image I realized that eyes are the symbol of a light portal, and science has discovered that cells within the physical body communicate via light. My feet, hands, and forehead were potential light conduits, and during the high kundalini flow, as they were being newly opened to this energy, they were reacting to the intense increase of light flow (photons) moving through my body. Resistance brought on by my issues and ignorance created the burning of the flesh on my feet and hands. The image of the White Tara points toward the awakened potential of what the human body is capable of manifesting. Light is a conduit of information. Today, over 40 years later, I am continuing to open to that flow and have experienced episodes with energy flows so strong that I am driven into a fetal position on the floor, thinking that this is the one that I won't survive. My legs now feel a vibrating coolness from the knees down. The center of my hands is always filled with a warm buzzing, and the universal sound current is constantly singing to me. My third eye allows me to see and know. Focusing on any of these aspects immediately increases the energy flow and can raise me out of my surrounding physical awareness.

The first time I built a pyramid was in 1973. I was using it to sleep and meditate in, and it moved everything into higher gear and became the inspiration for the one that sent me over the edge years later. However, I had a couple of powerful experiences during that time which are worth sharing. One warm summer day, I was walking along a stream in the woods with two friends when we came across a 10-inch diameter tree that had grown horizontally over the stream. It had been cut off eight or nine feet out, so I walked to the end and was trying to balance. My two friends decided it would be fun to shake me off into the stream. I love to play, so after hitting the water, I got out and ran out to the end of the log for another go at it. This became the game: Shake Greg off into the water. After a few times, though, something in me shifted, and instead of me experiencing their hands shaking the long stump, I had the sensation that all the movement was coming from me. My feet were shaking their hands through this eight-foot pole. When I felt myself as the source of all the movement, nothing could knock me off. In this moment, I deeply experienced the realization that when I am united with Source, and everything is coming from me, I am totally responsible for and in total control of my reality. There is nothing in Universe that can victimize me because I am Universe in expression.

A few days later, I took this even deeper when a fellow meditator asked me if I ever had dreams where I was falling and then woke up with a jolt when I hit. Before I go on with this story, I need to share that years later, I learned that this is a widespread experience, and it comes from people "falling" back into their bodies from traveling in the astral planes at night. This was verified in an interesting way by a neighbor of mine who had an 18-month-old daughter who always woke up crying. Her half-sister, who was 17 years old, could see people's energy bodies. One day as she was sitting next to her sleeping baby sister, she saw her descending energy body come back into her physical body, which was facing up. The mother had gotten into the pattern of turning her young daughter over on her back as she slept. She thought it would help her breathe better, but the baby girl came back from the astral dream world into her body face down, reversed from her physical orientation, and became very angry and confused. Enlightened by this insight, the mother then allowed her young daughter to spend her time sleeping on her stomach, and she always woke up happy and smiling after that revelation. The more I have learned of events like this on the path toward higher consciousness, the more my scientific mind has been blown.

Back to my friend's question on falling in a dream and awakening suddenly: He told me that if I remembered to meditate as I was falling that I would never hit! Wow, that excited me. Sure enough, that next night I had a "falling" dream, and I remembered in my dream to meditate. I took off flying and was totally jazzed when I awoke. The best part, though, was the following night when I had a dark dream where I was being chased on a train by a bunch of bad guys. As I was running through one of the train cars, I remembered my experience in my previous night's dream. I sat down in the middle of the train car and started meditating. The train disappeared, the bad guys disappeared, and that was the last negative dream I had. That was over 50 years ago. To become aware and shift the scenario during the dream state empowers us to be conscious all the time regardless of our circumstance.

I now took the power of my log experience into the subconscious realm as well as the aware, "awake" state. I began to see that they are both totally malleable and interchangeable and that I am the creator. There is actually little difference between dreaming and waking, as far as malleability goes, except that one changes a little more quickly and easily. My night and day reflect each other as it became possible to be conscious within the supposed subconscious and in both, I am learning not to take my projection too personally or too seriously. The key is to be fully present and conscious. At this point in my life, I began to experience more fully the nature of our 3D reality as an illusion. I traveled the world at night and sometimes felt that I accomplished more work while I was out of my physical body than when I was in it and awake to this 3D reality.

I have realized that I am most powerfully supported when I clearly choose to be of service to all, and I'm humble enough to accept standing under a higher flow of wisdom that could be poured into me as I emptied myself of my preconceived ideas. I discovered that intelligence is more than the accumulation of information or a measure of how much I can store and recall from my head. I became aware that anything that I wished to know can be found on the higher/inner planes of our being.

I realized that I had created the drama of my kundalini awakening as a learning. I chose this path and form of awakening and was never really in jeopardy from the energy. Over a couple of years, the roller coaster ride softened, and the energy smoothed out. I stopped all reading during that time to avoid influencing the information that was flooding into me. I didn't spend time around TVs or radios, finding them disruptive. I built what my guidance showed me and what I remembered from other lives and other places. They allowed it to occur by discovery, like a small child learning to color. The depth of love rising from Source, even a drop of it, was ecstatic, and it was the purpose for living. My connection was becoming very clear and strong. I could feel when I was asking incorrectly or when I was to pursue a different track. I had dozens of beings supporting me to proceed with the work that needed to be done.

I shared what I was building out of welded metal with others, and the lingering scientist in me was always amazed when they reacted positively, feeling the energy flow from a shape made out of bronze. I came to understand that what I was working with was known as Sacred Geometry. I learned that these forms were tools that acted as antenna systems collecting, organizing, and rebroadcasting higher dimensional, natural energy that could be felt and interacted with. The archetypal forms that I was mimicking were coherent fields of energy resonant with the three-dimensional angles of each physically created form. Like a C tone setting a C tuning fork into sympathetic resonance, these physical forms created from blueprints of the pre-physical could move someone into vibratory connection with the higher realms of creation to find their own path of discovery with the possibility of stepping into similar fields of purity as I had come upon.

In the spring of 1985, I walked into the garage of the old ashram. I had sold the house a number of months before but still had a dining room table stored there, and I was checking on it. Leaning against the table was a stack of large paintings and standing next to them was the artist. She introduced herself as a friend of the new owner, who had offered her a place to paint. The conversation was moving smoothly, so I pulled my box of geometric forms out of the car and shared them with her. She asked if I knew Bucky Fuller, and when I said I didn't, she invited me to a channeling that she was conducting with a friend, bringing in the spirit of Bucky. The energy coming through that evening expressed excitement over the geometries I was sharing. Bucky spoke about making them larger and shining colored lights through them onto people inside—but if one wasn't careful, he said, you could "fry someone like an egg."

Synchronicity is a divine aspect of Universe letting you know that you are loved and on the right track. In 1984, the year before I met Gail, I was handed a business card during a workshop and told I should connect with this person. I was told only a few of these handmade cards, with a photograph of a colorful abstract painting glued on the front, were handed out. I wrote "sound/ color/meditation" on it and stuck it in my wallet with good intentions. It was the only card I carried for over a year, and after a short while of dating Gail, I pulled it out of my wallet and asked, "This is you, isn't it?"

I was 38 and had never been inclined toward marriage, but with Gail, it was different. We knew we had a mission together, and marriage was the next step to manifest our love and potential. We were greater together than apart; synergy, a word coined by Bucky, was pulling us toward something greater.

CHAPTER 1
WHAT IS CONSCIOUSNESS?

I've been witnessing the progress of an eggplant seed I planted last week, experiencing the joy of watching this vulnerable, tiny sprout courageously poke through the soil in the little peat pot and begin its journey into becoming a productive vegetable plant. What a miracle that this offspring from a plant I will never know has gifted me with the possibility of life that can provide me nourishment! And yet this miracle is something more. This seed embodies codes that have been evolving for tens of thousands of years, part of a plant kingdom, a lifeforce energy that contains the plan, needs, spirit, and consciousness of life itself.

All these seeds, the DNA of humans and animals, the way rocks and minerals are formed, and even the way the wind blows have explicit structure, purpose, and consciousness. Our relationship with these things is energy. Everything begins as pure energy that finds its way into the physical world, holding within it a spirit of divine potential—or consciousness. Without consciousness, there is no lifeforce, no direction, no purpose to the essential breath we are often not even aware of. Consciousness is the container and structure of all that is. The unified field. The oneness we seek. It is planted in the structure of our being.

Consciousness is everywhere and can't be seen. We only become aware of the effects that consciousness offers in our lives. We live in a world where we pay more attention to physical objects, yet our feelings, inspirations, and journey to manifest meaning and purpose create a drive within to grasp the spiritual nature of life and understand our place within this physical realm, which is an offshoot of consciousness.

Sometimes people use the word *awareness* interchangeably with the word *consciousness*. However, these words are distinctly different. Awareness draws on the capability to use our brains, our senses, and the sentient body we have in order to experience our perceptions of what appears to be happening within and without us. Through that information, we build our own unique reality and view what we call awareness. The more that we exercise and utilize awareness, it expands and is fine-tuned to be more capable of navigating our inner and outer selves. We become convinced of its "truth," yet there is no absolute truth to awareness since each one of us have our own unique experiences and filters that determine how we perceive what lies within and without.

Awareness is a subset of consciousness, with consciousness enveloping everything. That is because it is God's self-talking to God's self—the unfolding of God's play.

What's distinctly different about consciousness is that it incorporates our awareness and unifies it with the spirit of all that is—or God consciousness. We cannot fully perceive consciousness because we are within it and the brain alone is incapable of fully grasping expanded multidimensional awareness. This is why so many people ponder their relationship with the divine. It's too huge for our linear intellect and requires that we become emersed in a deep state that journeys into the evolving enormity of life itself. Consciousness invites us into the realm of our spiritual journey, aligned with everlasting love. To understand consciousness, we wrestle with divine aspects of knowledge at the root of all creation.

Consciousness is basically synonymous with what we refer to as God, Creator, Source, and Unity, and it is expressed in every aspect of creation. To expand our sphere of consciousness, to allow it to be more inclusive of potentially all that is, we must step out of a limited awareness and utilize higher senses.

Native elders honor the consciousness within a stone, animals, plants, nature, and indeed all existence. They listen through the heart and spirit to commune deeply and communicate with all life forms. They were taught to expand their awareness to recognize the dignity of their world and experience how their personal lives are directly linked to all life around them.

Evolving our consciousness is one of the highest paths possible; we can choose to communicate and play with Unity for the higher good of all. We can be part of an evolutionary change that is overtaking humanity at this time, as transformational energies flood our planet, solar system, and Universe.

Most importantly, this is a time when each one of us has the opportunity to understand how we can participate with this energy that we're calling consciousness and engage from our soul, heart, and from the essence of all living substance. When we experience consciousness as pure energy, then we can grow expansively since everything is energy, and consciousness is an energetic expression of all life.

THE GOD SPARK

We will show you in this book how consciousness goes from the pure realm of energy to form matter, and the more it is aligned with its source of creation, the more it is in the perfection of the intent of what created it—the God spark.

Consciousness is the creative force, the spark of all truth within all aspects of creation as everything is being drawn back into unity from which it is birthed.

Ultimately, consciousness can be understood as the source of everything in our reality. This may be the most important time to be alive to expand your consciousness and allow the God spark to be expressed through your life. We are more than just this physical body and personality that we see looking back at us in the mirror. That personality may seem to be caught up in trying to survive in this world with the most comfort and least pain. What is that aspect of us that's drawing us to something greater? It's consciousness awakening within us, pushing the boundaries of what we experience as our reality. We often use the metaphor that we are like an iceberg because, like an iceberg, only a small percentage of us is seen. The majority of the iceberg is hidden underneath the water and is totally invisible to anybody in a boat floating past.

Likewise, with human beings, much more exists beyond the realm of the physical senses. One of the first levels out from the physical is our emotional body. Some people have expanded their visual acuity into this realm and have the ability to see colors around a person that reflect their emotional state. This energy field is referred to as the aura and is recognized by many ancient healing traditions. The electrical potential of this field can be measured with scientific equipment and is found around plants, animals, and all living organisms. Although this is another dimension that is invisible to most of us, we still feel it in our bodies and we describe it as "feeling our emotions." Even though we feel them, we may not recognize and manage how they're interacting with our body and the world around us. By evolving consciousness, it is possible to work with this invisible part of ourselves. By incorporating a higher, more complete view of the emotional body, we can become masters of our emotions, rather than sometimes feeling victimized by them.

Like the hidden part of our iceberg metaphor, if we expand further into the invisible field surrounding each of us, we come across the mental body where thought forms are held and travel. Those people who can see into the dimensions of a person recognize that thought forms have an energetic quality that can remain with us for a long period of time. These thought forms cloud our ability to see the world clearly because they filter current happenings through old thought patterns from past experiences and perspectives that are triggered and activated inside the brain from the mental body. The mental body is an aspect of ourselves through which we can learn to master how our conscious and unconscious thoughts are working. Viewing our thoughts before they become actions, or before they come out of our mouths, allows us to choose our words more carefully and gain perspective of the hidden elements that are also in play.

This higher perspective of the mental body is an essential teaching of East Indian and Buddhist philosophies, where they speak of the mental impressions as samskaras, which are a basis for the development of karma theory. They believe if we are unable to expand into greater recognition within the mental realm and release the limiting views that mold our view of reality, we will be cursed to repeat our mistakes and misunderstandings to live a painful and unsatisfactory life.

When we are caught in the past, we have a limited sense of present experience and can easily miss the fresh, new gift being offered in the moment. By expanding into the various dimensions represented by the iceberg, we can gain access all the way up to the level of soul, a level that cultivates the expression of truth. At the physical level, where we spend much of our focus, understanding is based on the transitory. Everything our senses interact with will change or die. This issue of impermanence is compounded by the fact that all information is filtered through our beliefs and judgements, which makes each person's understanding of reality totally unique. No great truths could ever be found here; they only exist at the highest levels of permanence. At the level of soul, we can move into a more permanent and fulfilling aspect of our being.

All these different aspects are dimensions that are unseen from the physical; however, by incorporating the fullness of our consciousness into awareness, we become capable of becoming masters, able to work with a greater playing field.

ICEBERGS, ACUPUNCTURE, MAGNETS, AND DEEP-SEA DIVERS

Here is an image of the iceberg we've been discussing where only the tiny bit at the surface is what most of us relate to as the whole iceberg. The analogy shows the reliance we place on the physical level, which limits our awareness and thus our ability to fully live life and evolve consciously.

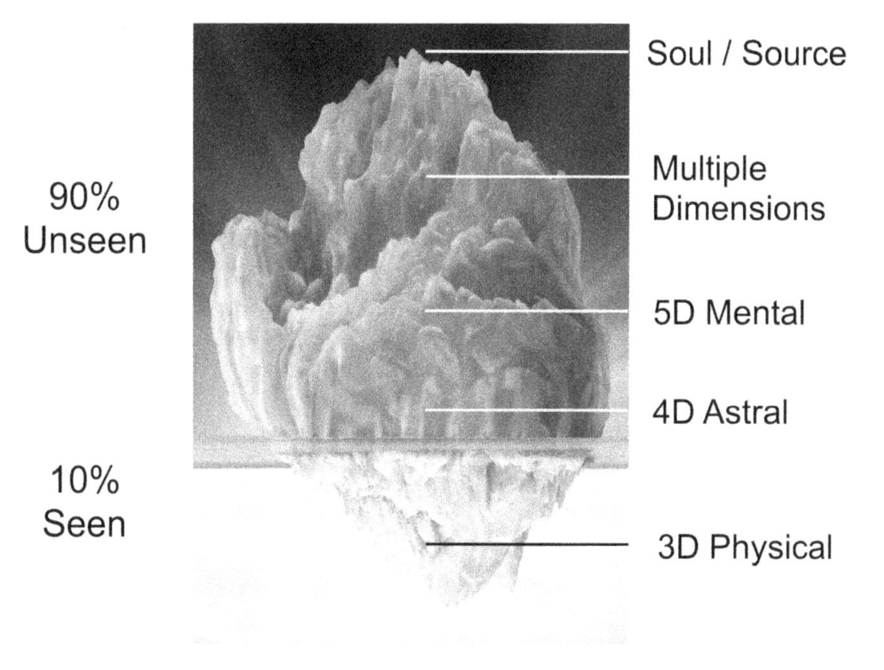

Fig. 1-1

To strengthen the metaphor, we've turned it upside down to offer a better perspective in understanding the hidden aspects that exist between the soul, which came first, and the physical dimension. Everything is created on the primary level of Source before it flows from the top initiating point through all levels of our being, finally coalescing in the density of the physical. We've layered it like a cake because that's easier for our linear minds to accept; however, the fact is, it's not linear. Nothing outside of our limited physical view of reality is linear in space or time. We show all those different aspects on the iceberg to describe the fullness of who we are.

It's a metaphor, though. Everything we're going to discuss in this book must be metaphorical because truth can't be captured by words. Truth is an experience. It's a feeling, a deep understanding that goes beyond all words. The words that we fall back on are the metaphors to say, "Life is like this." The iceberg metaphor shares an understanding of how dependent we are on our higher consciousness and soul for our existence. When we speak about multiple dimensions, the dimension that is closest to our body is often referred to as the etheric. It exists within a few inches of the physical body and is the energetic interphase between the solid matter and subtle fields of energy that surround us. It's the energetic link to the fourth dimension where the colorful emotional body is displayed.

An acupuncturist follows detailed maps of energy points on the body. By activating specific points with inserted needles they can increase energy flow where there had been blockage or inadequate flow before. Have you ever noticed how long some of their needles are? There is a reason for that. Needles act as small antenna towers collecting energy. By being longer than an inch, they are able to pierce the etheric field of the body and create a siphon effect with the fourth dimension, using the energy of the etheric body as a driver to open the flow of energy from the higher realms. When that energy flows, the physical body can receive healing and become balanced with the help of the energy input by moving fourth-dimensional energy into the physical body.

Another way that acupuncturists stimulate energy points is by placing magnets on them. Simply put, magnets are made by combining particular metals, then heating and running a strong electrical current through them. This creates an internal molecular geometry that allows "magnetic" energy to flow. Science has no consensus in understanding what this energy flow is. They simply refer to it as "magnetic" energy. From a higher perspective it is etheric energy, a cross-over energy flow between the physical and subtle bodies. Magnets work in a similar way as needles, stimulating a flow of etheric energy, which then directs fourth-dimensional energy into acupuncture points needing activation. The south pole of a magnet, where the energy is flowing out, is the end that is usually directed toward the body.

When properly used, the etheric energy directed through the magnet can stimulate healing activity within the body. It's important to work carefully because if left on too long, it may create an imbalance in the direction of overload, too much energy. If the body is out of balance, think of it like a seesaw, where one side is raised, and one side is lowered. You could bring energy in to press the raised side down until the other side starts coming up. The proper timing is critical to remove the magnet when balance is achieved, rather than allowing it to stay and force the other side of the seesaw up too high, causing imbalance. Whenever working with energy, balance is important to achieve.

Let's consider another metaphor, that of the deep-sea diver. The boat on the surface of the water is pumping him life supporting oxygen and is similar to what is represented in the iceberg metaphor as the Source or soul at the top. Source is moving energy through all the different dimensions and through the different levels of the ocean until it reaches the deep-sea diver at the bottom in his pressurized suit. He wears heavy leaded boots to keep from floating up to the surface; likewise, each of us is surrounded by heavy negative emotions that act as a weight keeping us stuck at the lowest level of our potential, the third dimension. We are dependent for our survival on our soul link, just as the deep-sea diver always needs to have a connection to his ship on the surface. Our soul is literally pumping our life force constantly to us. If the soul were to be taken out of the picture, we would immediately die, just like a deep-sea diver whose air has been cut off. The way in which the energy flows from Source all the way into our lives is an important aspect to discuss because that's where we get into creating resonance with soul and exploring ways to increase that flow of energy. It's most important to realize that energy is flowing and needs to flow into our lives all the time.

Fig. 1-2

AWAKENING TO THE NATURAL ORDER OF CREATION

As we move into a relationship with the bigger part of our being, we discover how wonderful life can be. From the higher perspective that is offered, 3D distractions become much smaller and less intimidating. We feel more in control as we watch our life journey with less emotional involvement: such as a parent watching their child play, we can observe without taking everything so personally. From the higher valley's edge, we can more easily recognize the path down the center of the valley, and the serendipities that start unfolding more rapidly become an expectation of how life is to be led when full connection is allowed to flow through the heart center into our daily life.

We begin to realize that all difficulty and disease are a result of blocking or denying this higher flow of energy from Source. As more doctors acknowledge that negative emotions and stress can influence a person's health, they are slowly recognizing the interactions we have with aspects of the fourth dimension (emotional realm) and fifth dimension (mental realm). Impediments that show up in these higher unseen dimensions influence the quality of life in our physical reality. In fact, this leads us farther down the rabbit hole of third-dimensional illusion toward the understanding that there are no causes at all in our third-dimensional reality. We exist in a dimension of effects *only.* All causes are initiated on higher dimensional levels of existence before they manifest in our everyday reality. Thus, if we wish to create true change in our lives, it is necessary to understand and claim these higher dimensional aspects where the source of our power and intelligence is generated.

This is where we go for our inspiration, for love, and to feel the wholeness of who we are. It's also where we go to expand our consciousness and realize who we truly are. Rather than on the physical level, the third-dimensional level is where we discover things by doing. However, doing can only take us to the limits of what the physical body is capable of. It's when we expand into the higher levels that we discover the fullness of our consciousness. This is why it's important to practice mindfulness, meditation, creative time, and disciplines that help us find the peaceful and quiet place within. This is sometimes referred to as the zero point, coming back to the core of who each one of us is to experience our beingness to balance with the doingness and physical stimulation we are so familiar with every moment of each day.

It's a significant part of our life to develop and master access to higher inspiration, listen to our intuition, advance our ability to recognize the wisdom available to us, build higher awareness outside ourselves as well as within, and integrate this into everyday life.

The balance is very important, and the lifeline that is presented to the deep-sea diver not only gives the diver the nourishment of the air that she needs, it gives the diver the ability to stay connected with her essence and soul. Without that, we're not a full-dimensional human.

The potential of where we're going by raising our consciousness can be expressed very simply by this story of a small bird known as the veery thrush, which nests in northern New England and southern Canada.

During the summer breeding season, these tawny-colored songbirds are dedicated to raising a brood of chicks. A scientist studying the veery thrush found that sometimes the timing of their cycle of nesting, raising young, bringing them into full adulthood, and then migrating changed from season to season. He tried to discover the elements that fed into this change. Why would they cut their important breeding season short? Was it a function of the availability of food that summer? Was it the density of the thrushes that lived in that particular area? He discovered that this bird wintered in Brazil in South America, which is a migration of over 4,000 miles to get to their winter habitat. Their migration route took them over the Gulf of Mexico, the large body of water between North and South America. The success of their migration was dependent on the quality of the weather over the Gulf. If a hurricane were to happen during their migration cycle, it would reduce their survival rate more than anything else. He learned that they abandoned their summer breeding grounds at a particular time to avoid hurricanes and severe weather in the Gulf. The veery thrush has been recorded at successfully noting the intensity of a hurricane season months in advance. Their accuracy in determining whether there would be hurricanes during their migration time or not was more accurate than the computerized models used by our modern weather service. It boggles the mind that the power of computers, collected data, and various information services that come through human mental capabilities could not match what this small bird can do with its tiny, measurable brain.

All the brilliant minds that had focused on the importance of weather prediction were outdone by a tiny "bird brain." We use the phrase "bird brain" to slander someone, so what is really going on here? When we think about where our intelligence lies, most people point to their heads. Many of us think our big brains are the center of our success—the character at the tip of our iceberg metaphor with the really big brain is creating and controlling everything else. It all flows forth from us, the one interacting with this physical world.

NOT SO.

This really begs the question of consciousness. It's not something that is dependent on mental capabilities but rather the source of all information and all being. When we are tapped into that larger part of ourselves, the part inclusive of higher consciousness, we have access to all the information that is of value to us in our life at the moment. If we wish to expand our life's needs to be of service to others, that information from consciousness is there for us, just as easily, as clearly, and definitely, as it is for the necessary life cycle of the veery thrush.

The reality of and dependence on this connection is demonstrated by many animals and plants that must be tuned into this level of awareness for their survival and to have their lives fully operational in relationship with the patterns and cycles of life on this planet. This is true throughout the entirety of this planet, the solar system, and Universe. Every part is interlinked and dependent upon every other. Science is now showing us that every aspect of Universe is tied to every other aspect of Universe. We are a part of this unity and become more aware of our connections when we raise our level of consciousness to the brilliance of existence provided for by the God source. We can be totally fulfilled and taken care of as easily as any flower or animal.

When we work with the order revealed by nature, we are fueled by the wisdom that's within those natural patterns. It's the heart, soul, and methodology of creation. When we align with these universal patterns, we overcome the pain and drama of separation that is so prevalent in our lives and our societies today. This is why we are writing this book: to offer you tools and understanding to navigate your life in a more conscious way, a more fulfilling and joyful way, by feeling the connection to all that is. You can evolve the ability to clearly reference the soul vibration and remember all parts of who you are so that you're able to overcome distractions. You will be enabled to move through the density in a way that you recognize that even though all these things are happening, they're not the defining factor. The true defining factor is your exquisite beingness. As with exercising a muscle, the more you work with that muscle, the more powerful and adept it becomes in supporting you to take on more and evolve to a higher order.

It's that higher order that every aspect of creation reflects. Birds know what it is to be the kind of bird they are. A plant embraces its limitations and its opportunities. We've discovered that plants do much more than we ever thought they were capable of. They give each other growing space and recognize proper timing and succession. They share minerals with other plants through their root systems. Trees and plants communicate through their root systems and can even warn each other of impending problems.

In essence, what we're sharing is that this is the natural order of creation. Animals, plants, and minerals know how to be what they are. It is the human being that has forgotten its humanness and misplaced its proclivity to be the fullness of who it is, unlike the small bird who can tap into the overall consciousness of what is and what will be.

It's the human being's time to awaken to that same potential and engage with the fulfillment of the natural rhythms that animals, plants, and everything in creation follow to achieve resonance and harmony.

We search everywhere within the "tip" of our iceberg experience for happiness, love, understanding, and a life of fulfillment. The physical life we are so accustomed to knowing as "reality" can never deliver on the higher aspects of creation because they don't fully exist here. We are only playing with 10 percent of possibility. The Source of all possibility, the Source of all love and all understanding radiates out from the highest aspects of our being. For this reason, spiritual masters have often referred to this reality as an illusion, impermanent and unable to satisfy our deeper needs. It is only by embracing the eternal core of our being that true happiness can be embodied in our lifetime.

All snowflakes are unique, yet when each one melts, it dissolves into the same ocean of water that is the essence of every other snowflake. Every human being has a unique physical world expression at the tip of their iceberg reality. However, all of us share the same underlying and expansive multidimensional nature. We all share the same restless desire to expand into the fullness of our being, a soul expressed through the human body, mind, and emotions. With higher insight and presence, the challenges and lessons at each dimensional level can be resolved. Energy blockages that had impeded the flow of Divine Source can be transformed, allowing love to flow into this 3D reality.

TAKE A MOMENT TO REFLECT . . .

We invite you on this journey to explore these natural rhythms and frequencies so that you might expand into the fullness of all that is by being resonant with all that you are.

We look at the world
and see many problems.
It is all illusion.

There is only one problem,
unconsciousness,
and only one solution—Consciousness.

The Truth is:
Consciousness doesn't come from the head.
It isn't found by thinking and doing.

It arises from being, flowing
Into creation through the heart.

—Gregory Hoag

CHAPTER 2
WHAT INHIBITS CONSCIOUSNESS?

If consciousness is the unified field, the context for all life, and planted in the structure of our being, what can possibly inhibit it?

Let's look at this question from the perspective of pure energy. Without movement and flow, there is no life, and biological functions cease. When an organism no longer accepts the intake of energy, its life ends. In other words, every living organism is dependent upon its connection to the field of energy. The sun is our major source of energy and if it ceases to exist, all life on our planet would also expire. The energy of the sun and our planetary system are often outside of our moment-to-moment awareness and can easily be taken for granted.

With climate change and many of the weather disasters we are experiencing, we are becoming more aware of our primary relationships. When we lack awareness of certain "givens," we become ill-adapted to our ecosystem and the patterns and cycles of life, which leads to decisions that cause long-term harm. We are learning about how our unconscious interactions with Mother Earth have precipitated degradation and destruction on our planet. The earth is an abundant living system that must be honored and conscientiously interacted with to maintain healthy and productive life for all. It is strongly dependent upon our consciousness and good flow of energy. When a lake becomes stagnant, it is in breakdown, entering a cycle of death, just as when we make decisions that have detrimental effects on the earth and each other.

Energy is infinite and is always in some mode of transformation, always constantly moving toward flow and balance, even if that triggers extreme situations. This is an important concept to explore.

We live in a rural area of northeastern Colorado on land near a small river. In September 2013, the river had been dry for a number of months, and fire danger was high due to several years of serious drought. We had been praying for much-needed rain and were delighted when the moisture finally appeared. We were having dinner with some dear friends and were thrilled to hear and smell the desired rain. It was a great relief. The rains continued and got stronger. As a matter of fact, there was a weather front that strengthened and stalled over us for days. Our little river, which had been a virtual mud puddle, returned and started swelling over its banks.

In the past, we had seen occasional strong rainy periods produce flooding and were familiar with how the water would spread over the surrounding land, always feeling grateful for the moisture. However, this weather pattern was different, as it strengthened and continued to release large amounts of precipitation, which was highly unusual for this ecosystem. The mountains and canyons above us were receiving unprecedented amounts of rain as well. As gravity was forcing the flow of water downhill and easterly, it created logjams in some of the canyons above us until there was enough force for an enormous and very destructive surge of water to take out everything in its way. Huge amounts of land, trees, and even homes were swept away by the violent force of the water we had been so happy to welcome back. We watched this shocking 1,000-year flood as it swept away many acres of our land and closed in on our homesite. We realized we were witnessing the forces of creation, and it called us to be present in each moment and take appropriate action—such as get the children, animals, and important things into the car and drive to our closest neighbor's home who was not in harm's way. We were at the mercy of nature and had no idea where this was leading us.

We had never experienced anything like this; however, because we have maintained our spiritual connections for many years, we were able to stay centered and connected. We sidestepped the fear and reluctance to accept this new reality and looked for creative solutions ("soulutions") to move forward. We had been doing a practice before this occurrence using the intention: "I am grateful for all that is coming." As morning came, we were able to see that our home was still standing; however, it was perched on a 30-foot cliff overlooking a very powerful and hugely swollen river. We lost the home's infrastructure, driveway, well, septic system, organic garden, and many acres of land. But the home itself was untouched. We felt shaken but knew inside that we were cared for.

As time went on, we repaired and rebuilt what was needed and learned to love and cultivate our new landscape. We both felt extraordinarily grateful to witness this evolution of earth and maintain our well-being.

Energy must flow, and consciousness is a key adjunct to this. We are creative beings with lives and the environment giving us feedback all the time. It's up to us to be aware and recognize the serendipity of each moment and choose how we are impacted by the energy. As we stay connected to our higher knowing, the flow continues; however, one of the big deterrents we each face is the human emotion of fear. Fear cuts off the flow. Fearlessness maintains our lifeline to soul. Fear is the antithesis of love, while love is the direct current. Fear poses the question of whether we are safe and can survive a situation, while love and trust offer us the balance and confidence to make positive decisions. Fear generates the need to control a situation to feel safe. Fear constructs an illusory idea that takes control of us.

As the story of the flood demonstrated, we cannot control external situations. We can, however, take control of our responses, actions, and perceptions. As we maintained our connection to a higher understanding, resolutions appeared, people and situations came forward, and we learned to love our new landscape even more than how it was before. There were many around us who continued to suffer from the fear they experienced and the pain of loss. We stayed centered, present, and recognized which choices served us best.

This crisis taught us the value of remaining connected and illuminated how easily fear and disconnection can block higher consciousness. The answers and gifts were outside of our control, beyond what we could see in the physical dimension, and remained in the realms of a loving spirit.

CYCLES OF LIFE

We've come to understand the cycles of life—seasons, aging, and deterioration, which offer us a perspective of breakdown. We watch our children grow from newborns to teenagers and adults. We plant trees and gardens and delight as they grow and offer us food and shade before they return to the earth for the next season. We intellectually understand the impermanence of life and have a range of emotional reactions that grapple with our personal journey.

Even though we enjoy celebrating another year circling the sun, it's still challenging and discomforting to look at ourselves in a mirror and see the aging facial lines appear along with graying hair and lack of resiliency. How can that be happening and what can be done to stop it or at least slow it down? It can happen so gradually that we don't notice, since we are engaged in continuous cycles, watching the signs of physical veneer slowly wearing thin. We understand our mortality, yet accepting the parameters and cycles of the physical world can be challenging. The physical world is coded to pass through cycles and breakdown for its long-term existence. It is the nature of physical life as a unity. Every action corresponds to reactions. To live a functional existence, it is necessary to grow our understanding of the multidimensional levels that all life exists on. When we are more comfortable with our universal connections, we have greater flexibility to navigate life and embrace a perspective that incorporates the wholeness of who we are.

Life gives us personal experiences that move us beyond stagnation and into the flow. As much as we'd love to hold onto a moment or era, it is impossible, and the opposite of what life flow is about. From the Soul perspective, we are not here to live a life of controlling and collecting experiences and resources. We are here to participate in this physical realm with deep love, appreciation, compassion, and creative expression.

The nature ingrained in each moment offers powerful new signals that can catalyze a stressful reaction when it is interpreted as interrupting something we are familiar with. Stress is often triggered by change and shows that something is no longer functioning optimally or has completed its cycle and is ready for change. Stress can be experienced as a positive or negative occurrence; it's completely up to the individual how it is perceived. Yet stress is another major factor that causes the blockage of energy and breakdown, even though it is a neutral and natural part of life. Most medical professionals designate stress as a leading cause of disease, mental health decline, and dysfunction in relationships. When stress progresses into fear it blocks the flow of energy.

Energy can be blocked and circumvented. Energy can be diverted and redirected. Acupuncture is an effective way to open blocked energy or chi by inserting needles into specific energy points on the body. The blockage can have a direct effect on the health and well-being of an individual. Without the flow of energy, life itself will cease to exist. When we observe the issue as an energetic constriction, it becomes easier to resolve. Furthermore, when we recognize the emotional issues and belief systems attached, we can initiate healing what caused this reaction. Becoming more conscious of the cycles prepares us to look for the places of refuge and connection that allow a new perspective to grow. Finding our modes to reconnect spiritually with nature, and each other, in meditation or other forms of mindfulness give us a path to find our center within the unity of life.

And why are we living in a system that makes the life force we need seem so vulnerable? We live in a physical world of impermanence, yet the eternal aspect of our soul is always there as our lifeline. Whenever our lifeline to the divine realm of consciousness is impinged upon, we are unable to fully connect to the wealth of who we are. Modern life is full of challenges to our health and well-being, including electromagnetic waves, toxins, and the technology we love that surrounds us. The social fabric is producing a time of extreme polarity that disrupts families, friendships, and governments. The use of addictive drugs and the suicide rate has grown to alarming proportions. As social media deeply affects the self-esteem of young people, it is evident we are in a state of extreme crisis.

THE MOST SERIOUS ISSUE WE FACE

What inhibits consciousness is the most serious issue that we face today, in part because we are unaware that it is an issue.

We look outward at a world that is breaking down in many areas and fail to see it reflects us. We are the ones breaking down. Our physical, emotional, and mental health is being constantly assaulted by the environments we are creating and are becoming more dysfunctional. We think we can overcome by creating solutions through advanced technology, but too frequently the solutions are often the source of our problems. We need a major reset as an intelligent species if we are to survive.

The awareness necessary for this reset must flow from the higher aspects of our being, that which we are unknowingly blocking and eliminating from everyday life. Reflected by the iceberg metaphor that we just shared, this means we are being forced into a reality and understanding found only within 10 percent of our full potential. As shared by Albert Einstein: "We cannot solve our problems with the same thinking we used when we created them." We have been trapped by limited 3D thinking, a thought process that separates us from each other and our environment with the understanding that we exist only within what we can see and touch. Without embracing our multidimensional nature, we are doomed.

Our current technology is based on this belief and creates modern "solutions" that are holding us to a pattern of degradation that only portends to get more dire. 99.99999 percent of everything is pure energy, but our attempts to retrieve or generate energy within our 3D paradigm is to break down wood, coal, oil, or an atom to release the infinitely small fraction of energy hidden inside. We are literally destroying our environment to release usable energy and the byproducts of this process are toxic ripples impacting the well-being of life on many levels. The negative aspects are high, while the energy gain is low. Electric vehicles and solar power reflect a similar imbalance.

They appear as a positive step forward, but there is more to consider in their full energy equation. Both forms of renewable energy are inefficient and prolong the trap instigated by the same limited 3D dependency. Solar is a chemical reaction, and wind is a mechanical leveraging of motion. While in use, they appear to be green, but the lithium mining for the batteries takes a high toll on human beings and the environment. Couple this understanding with the cost of building both wind turbines and solar panels compared to their return and the difficulty in recycling or disposing of the short-lived technology at the end of their life cycle, and it becomes evident that they are not capable of offering a solution to our energy dilemma. They account for only 20 percent of our electricity, while the rest is still generated by breaking atoms and burning fossil fuels.

To syphon the unlimited energy underneath or beyond all this requires an interdimensional energy flow from outside of our physical system (zero-point technology). Staying within our physical realm for energy production is not sustainable and has negative consequences. The solutions most likely exist now, but what is lacking is the level of consciousness needed to share them with the world. Our societies, governments, and economies are based on separation, control, and fear. The belief systems and judgements that are maintaining this field are the first obstacles that must be overcome before the more enlightened views of unity, love, and service to all allows for true interdimensional technologies to take hold on this planet.

The first step for each of us is to work on ourselves. A single coherent being filled with love becomes empowered to hold the space for tens of thousands caught in the unfocused chaos of fear. This understanding has led to the belief that true change can indeed be ushered in by only a small percentage of the whole.

Consciousness is a flow of energy that attempts to move through the entirety of our multidimensional being, sustaining and aligning every aspect with the divine codes of perfection. The purpose of the iceberg metaphor was to emphasize the size of our higher dimensional self, which is over 90 percent of our being and the fact that Soul energy flows through these higher levels first before energizing our physical body. Existing within a free will Universe, we have the choice to believe anything we choose and judge our reality. This grants each of us the power to deny or block the higher flows of consciousness.

Most of us are unaware of how our emotional and mental bodies also participate in our isolation from the divine patterns of creation that flow from the higher levels, which are crucial for our health and well-being. From the moment of birth, our 3D awareness (ego) starts focusing on survival, on the things we need and the things to avoid. The main feedback mechanism for this process is called our emotional body, and it exists on the fourth-dimensional level of our being. The emotional body is full of colors for those who have developed that higher ability to see the human aura, but for most of us, it is invisible.

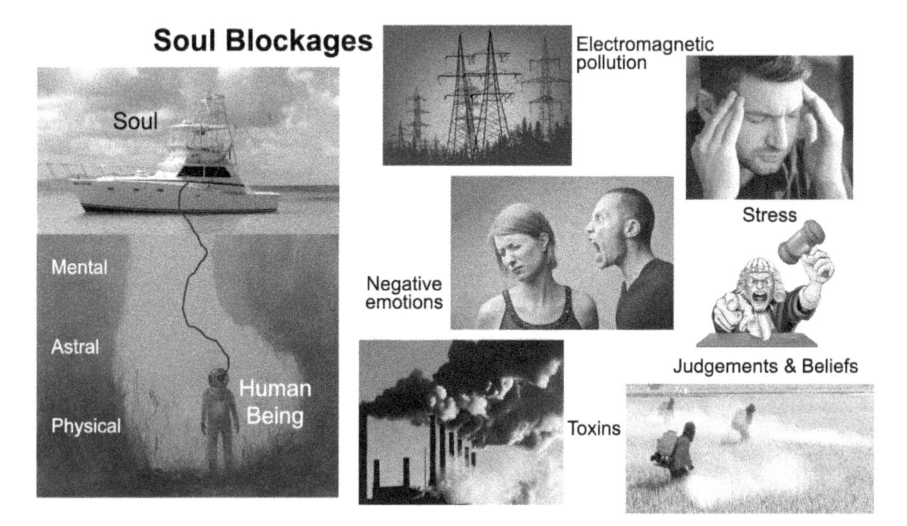

Fig. 2-1

It exists very close to our physical body creating a cocooning effect with its field of energy surrounding us. There are two distinct sources that input information into this field. What comes from the body are the survival mechanisms with some referred to as the fight or flight response, which is fear generated. What we may not realize is that all emotional responses from the physical body, such as anger, hate, sadness, and guilt, are forms of fear, which create a very thick field around the body that is difficult for the higher dimensional flows to penetrate.

The other inputs into this field come from the higher self and Soul. These are the inputs generating love, joy and connection, the feelings of attraction for something or someone. This is how the higher aspects of our being direct us toward the individuals and projects that benefit our life path. The difficulty is that the lower emotions of fear generated by the physical body are thick and heavy, not allowing the higher aspects of consciousness to easily pass through undistorted.

The mental body in the fifth-dimension keeps this field dense by constantly focusing on past injuries and fears or worrying about these same issues being repeated in the future. The physical body is unable to distinguish past, present, or future as it reacts equally to all fears and worries that are input into our emotional field by our active mental body. It also doesn't gauge severity very well. Without the balancing influence of a higher perspective, the emotional body stimulates the physical body with adrenaline, whether it's a saber-toothed tiger walking over the hill or your cat throwing up on the carpet before guests arrive.

> **All diseases and difficulties in the physical dimension reflect blocked or denied flows of energy from Source.**

On its own level the mental body plays a major role in stopping the wisdom of Soul from coming through. A runaway mind is constantly moving in so many convoluted directions that it ties itself into thick knots of stress by focusing on daily problems and difficulties. Again, this blocks the flow of consciousness and the divine archetypes of perfection that are the blueprints for health and well-being. This is why science views stress as a trigger for disease and the emotions of fear and anger generated within the emotional body can become the cause of cancer and degenerative conditions. All diseases and difficulties in the physical dimension reflect blocked or denied flows of energy from Source.

BEYOND A CULTURE OF FEAR

Fears run rampant in our world and are effectively used by politicians and powerbrokers to control people. Their rhetoric stimulates fears within the emotional body, creating thick walls around each person, depriving them of coherent, inclusive thinking that comes from a higher self. Without the influx of love and compassion, we are witnessing a rise in sociopathic behavior and a growing sense of separation as many of us are unable to connect to the Source of all love and happiness within the core of our being. The problems on the outside show us where we need to focus internally.

We don't realize how deeply we're steeped in this culture of fear. People are constantly approaching our business, Metaforms, for tools to protect them from EMFs (electromagnetic frequencies), but protection is based in fear. *Protection creates the need for protection.* Instead, the solution is higher connection. Raise your energy field into higher resonance so the negative aspects growing in the physical dimension can't block the true source of energy, then you are vibrating on a higher level of consciousness. You are operating from a higher dimensional aspect of your being. As paraphrased from John 17 in the Bible – You can be in the world, but not of it.

The portal into the body from higher dimensional realms and our doorway back to them is through our heart center, which is the central chakra or energy center of the body. It is near the physical heart, so people often confuse the two. Talking of "heart wisdom" or the phrase "listen to your heart" is not what it appears to be. Science has found that the heart has its own intrinsic nervous system, and it sends more information to the brain than the brain does to the heart, but this doesn't mean that it plays a major role in our guidance. The physical heart is not the source of all the information and support that is talked about; rather, it rests next to the chakra with the same name, which is the doorway to what can take on that role.

As we develop stronger relationships with the higher dimensional aspects of our being we discover that even our brains are not the source and repository of our wisdom. On the higher levels we have universal access to knowledge that supports our well-being and growth when we allow Source energy to flow and align the subtle aspects of our dimensional bodies with divine archetypes. Our potential growth and spiritual evolution lie in activating and creating a coherent relationship with the higher vibrational parts of our being that exist on other dimensional levels.

> **It's time to release the phrase "from the heart" and replace it with "through the heart."**

All thoughts, feelings, and actions begin first on the higher dimensional levels before moving into the physical dimension. There are no causes in this physical dimension, only effects. If we want to be in control of our life, if we want to be creative, if we want to be filled with the love and joy that never dies, then we need to integrate the biggest part of ourselves where all these potentials exist.

Human beings have been struggling with forging these higher relationships for thousands of years, but eventually something changed. We have entered an accelerated cycle of growth and, with the way Universe seems to balance energies, we are also witnessing an expanding impediment to that growth. We need to recognize the play that is unfolding and choose the best path forward personally and for the good of all.

> **In times when there were no electrical currents, when the air was not swarming with electrical influences, it was easier to be human. For this reason, in order to be human at all today it is necessary to expend much stronger spiritual capacities than was necessary a century ago.**

This is a very powerful statement, and it is even more striking when we understand who said it and when. This was shared in a lecture by Rudolf Steiner in 1917. He was a brilliant Austrian philosopher and the founder of Waldorf Education. He understood the workings of our higher dimensional bodies and was clear on the issues facing our spiritual growth. The dramatic shifts that he witnessed in human beings due to electrical currents were occurring only 24 years after Nikola Tesla lit up the Chicago World's Fair in 1893. There was almost no electricity at the time Steiner spoke compared to the overload of electrical frequencies that we have over one hundred years later, ranging from radio waves to microwaves and X-rays.

Notice how he phrased his concern that "it was easier to be human" before the invasion of electrical currents. Our humanness, our compassion, and our wisdom come from integrating the higher dimensional aspects of our being into our physical expression, and Steiner realized that electrical frequencies were blocking this process. Changes start happening in the subtle energy bodies long before they are evident in the physical body, so healthcare that is only focused on physical difficulties missed many of the correlations.

Steiner also alluded to the fact that it was much easier to connect to the higher spiritual realms a century before his time. What coincides with that assessment is the start of the Industrial Revolution in the 1800s. Earlier in this chapter we referenced the toxic ripples spreading out from our technologies; well, this is when it started. Smoking chimneys and dead rivers became a sign of progress. There was a massive shift from living on farms aligned with the rhythms of nature to cramped and unhealthy city dwelling. Factory workers stepped in time with assembly lines and with the advent of the electric light the natural cycles of the sun were lost, downshifting the health of our hormonal system that was linked to these natural rhythms.

Today we have microplastics and toxins running through our bloodstream and daily interaction with computers, smartphones, and 5G run homes. All of this disrupts our connections to the higher aspects of our being resulting in deteriorating physical, emotional, and mental health. We are experiencing rising sociopathic behavior, infertility, new diseases, and a stressed mindset driven by separation and fear.

> **The solution is not to abandon what we've created, which would be impossible, but to recognize the issue**

and start including technologies and wisdom that would offer energetic balancing.

All these negative effects are based on disconnection from the flow of Source energy and the resulting lack of consciousness. The solution is not to abandon what we've created, which would be impossible, but to recognize the issue and start including technologies and wisdom that would offer energetic balancing. We start by fostering our own higher connections and then expand outward in service to all.

The rest of this book is dedicated to this solution through the wisdom of Sacred Geometry because it is a universal language that is spoken on every dimensional level of our being. We can draw upon its elements to construct technologies based on harmonic resonance, like a "C" tuning fork that vibrates with a "C" tone. We can create relationships with the higher dimensional realms, allowing energy flow into our third-dimensional lives and establishing Divine alignment.

We will start with the numbers 1 through 9, sharing their qualities as building blocks, and then in later chapters show how to use them in the construction of 3D geometries that add the energetic pulse of a divine archetype to the environment.

TAKE A MOMENT TO REFLECT . . .

Living a healthy and prosperous life depends on embracing our multidimensional nature and keeping the channels open to the energy flow that connects us to our higher selves. As we stay connected to our higher knowing, the flow continues; however, the human emotion of fear cuts off this essential flow. At this time, fear is running wild on this planet, severing our lifeline to the consciousness of love and compassion. Fearlessness maintains our lifeline to Soul. Fear is the antithesis of love, while love is the direct current.

We live in a physical world of impermanence, yet we can depend upon the eternal aspect of our Soul that is always available as our lifeline. Whenever our lifeline to the divine realm of consciousness is impinged upon, we are unable to fully connect to the wealth of who we are. By recognizing and embracing the light of Soul, we come back home and into balance.

When we feel stressed or ungrounded, it is a signal to reconnect through the heart center, which is the central chakra of the body. When we feel pain, the body reminds us that it is asking to be bathed in love. When fear overtakes a situation, it indicates the connection to Soul needs restoring.

By understanding the basic principles of creation and its beauty, we unite with the higher vibrational parts of our being that exist on other dimensional levels. This is a very practical way to learn who we are and how to navigate life with wisdom and the bounty of what is here on this physical plane for us to enjoy. And in the spirit of joy, we infuse life with love and evolve.

CHAPTER 3
1 AND 2 THE DIVINE MASCULINE AND FEMININE

You do not belong to you. You belong to Universe. The significance of you will remain forever obscure to you, but you may assume you are fulfilling your significance if you apply yourself to converting all your experience to the highest advantage of others. Make the world work for 100 percent of humanity in the shortest possible time through spontaneous cooperation. Without ecological offense or the disadvantage of anyone. Nature is totally efficient, a self-regenerating system. If we discover the laws that govern this system and live synergistically within them, sustainability will follow and humankind will be a success. Never forget that you are one of a kind. Never forget that if there weren't any need for you in all your uniqueness to be on this earth, you wouldn't be here in the first place. And never forget, no matter how overwhelming life's challenges and problems seem to be, that one person can make a difference in the world. In fact, it is always because of one person that all the changes that matter in the world come about. So be that one person.

— R. Buckminster Fuller[3]

---

3 R. Buckminster Fuller. (n.d.). AZQuotes.com. Retrieved May 16, 2023, from AZQuotes.com Website: https://www.azquotes.com/author/5231-R_Buckminster_Fuller.

Each of us has an important role to play. The Soul journeys into the physical realm with exquisite capability and gifts. It is up to each individual to reach the resonance that enables those talents to be revealed and nurtured. Through all the twists and turns in our lives, we grapple with experiences that can lead us astray and eventually resolve issues to gain the deeper connection we long for. The answers we seek are reflected in our physical lives; however, the causes are all held in higher dimensions. As we better understand energy and resonance, we are equipped with tools that give choices to attract what we want into our lives. This chapter will help you recognize who you really are and how to navigate life with your soul at the helm.

We live in a world of creative potential that travels a scale from dark to light, despair to joy, confusion to clarity. Frequency measures how the energy vibrates. and resonance occurs when there is similarity that enables transfer of energy. When you walk into a room that feels joyful, your mood takes on those feelings if you are open to receiving that state. When you spend more time around people who are financially successful, your chances of being more successful rise. The resonance of energy serves to align you with various qualities to choose from. Understanding how energy creates life is analogous to receiving the operating guide for planet Earth.

Pure energy is formless, yet it is in a state of evolution, prepared to take on shape and function in specific patterns that we see all around us. These patterns are archetypes or models that form the structure and guiding principles for all life that can be animated by consciousness. You can find these archetypes everywhere, and they have existed since before creation evolved. These archetypes form the templates for creation and are carriers of pure energy. When we use these archetypes in things we build and create in our environment, they imbed patterns, numbers, and shapes that create resonance with Source. This offers us the potential to resonate or vibrate with the essence of creation and everything that surrounds us. When we start vibrating with the essential building blocks of life, we are open to the larger aspects of who we are, and this allows us to reach deeper levels of awareness and touch that consciousness.

All our work with Sacred Geometry is based upon this understanding for the purpose of building tools that activate higher awareness and interaction. In the mid-1980s we began intuitively making sacred geometrical structures, following inner guidance and artistic principles. We were surprised to feel how these "forms" radiated energy and helped people feel more connected, meditate more deeply and were being used for a myriad of health benefits. The creative process inspired us to learn more about how and why this worked so we could serve in higher capacities.

We are living in a deeply transformative time. The increasing energy of our environment is compelling us to look at our lives, how we show up in each present moment, and how we can positively impact life. Everything that we do is affected by consciousness. The more we interact consciously with Unity, even though we're all individuals, we experience being part of the whole.

We are embodied spirit and contain the potential to affect everything on this planet. As the veils between dimensions become thinner, we're seeing more of the immediate and long-term impact of our consciousness and the lack of it on the world. This offers us a compelling reason to be more in charge of how we relate to ourselves as fully conscious beings on a conscious planet, in a conscious Universe interacting with everything in creation.

Exploring these universal archetypes will expand your consciousness and help you create what you're desiring. By looking through the lens of an expanded perspective, you gain power and clarity to accept everything Universe offers.

UNIVERSAL PATTERNS OF NUMBER

All physical matter is made up of atoms, which in turn are made up of smaller subatomic particles—protons, neutrons, electrons, etc. Science tells us that 99.99999 percent of each atom is pure energetic space, while the actual physical matter represented by the subatomic particles amounts to only 0.00001 percent. This pure energy drives everything in Universe. That large percentage is not referring to the tangible physical matter we most often consider. Instead, it is everything that is held in the field of consciousness. Our challenge is that we focus our attention mostly on the

0.00001 percent that we can see, touch, and bump into. Physical reality is an extremely small part of the makeup. The majority of everything is pure energy. When we wrap our minds around that, we start to discover the process used by Source to construct this physical reality.

> ***The day science begins to study non-physical phenomena, it will make more progress in one decade than in all the previous centuries of its existence.***
>
> ***—Nikola Tesla***

This massive source of energy creates templates that precede the physical dimension and what we know as reality. We call these templates, or patterns, *Sacred Geometry*, and they are held in the field of consciousness. Sacred Geometry reflects how energy moves and displays itself at slower vibrational rates, which becomes all we see, hear, and touch.

> *A Little Story from Gregory*
>
> *I remember back in the 1980s how excited I was to learn about experiments with Kirlian photography. Researchers were able to photograph a leaf that had its tip cut off, and an energetic image of the entire leaf was seen on the photographic plate. Like Jell-O poured into a mold, the physical leaf had an energetic template to follow. Since we interpret things based on what we can see, we might look at the remaining bit of leaf and*

believe that the physical leaf created the energy field that appeared on the photographic plate. In part, it did, as organic growth is an interactive process directed by the energy archetypes and the variations in growth of the plant that stimulate the next unfolding of the energy template.

We are surrounded in this reality by a universal language. If you could go to the other side of Universe and communicate with someone from another planet or star system, you could use this language of pattern, rhythm, and cycle, and they could understand what you would be sharing with them. This is the language of Sacred Geometry. This is the power of Universal order.

Perhaps even more consequential is the fact that this Universal language moves through all the dimensional levels as well. This means that the non-physical phenomena that Tesla was referencing can be understood and manipulated through the language of Sacred Geometry. Also, the difficulties and blockages that each of us experience on these subtle realms, as shared in the previous chapter, are accessible to be worked with using sacred geometric tools, which have the power to interact on these higher, non-physical dimensions.

We find that everything—flowers, seashells, plants, animals—follows the immutable order of creation.

Fig. 3-1

The beautiful patterns in Fig. 3-1 show us the way the energy is activated to precisely form a variety of many different things. It's extraordinary and exquisite that everything varies, from each snowflake to each cabbage or sunflower. They all have something in common with what is derived from their energetic archetype. And yet, just like human beings, every single one is unique. However, the archetype anchors the consciousness that is held in a precise pattern with a connection to each aspect of creation.

We are living in a time that emphasizes duality and separation, which masks our underlying connections. Seeing these patterns helps us remember who we are in relation to everything outside of us. Yes, we have our own individuality, and yet we are not separated from the essence, the core of who we are, which is consciousness, the Spirit that created us all.

By acknowledging that everything is connected through consciousness, we have access to extraordinary knowledge. When we're aware of those higher levels, we're able to ask questions and get answers without having to go through the trial-and-error method. Many great discoveries have sprung from dreams and intuitive vision. Accessing higher guidance can become more commonplace with a supportive, energetic environment and mindset.

> ***A Little Story from Gail***
> *I like to work with Spirit by asking that I be shown something or receive a form of encouragement. This morning, I was asking Spirit to provide some signs if it was appropriate for me to go through with a project I'm involved with. And I wanted very specific signs. I made the request and let it go. Within a few hours, I got direct feedback in the form of several communications that showed me I am on track. I rely on this support to guide me and have trained myself to be watching for the signs that easily appear, but can also be missed, because they are sometimes very subtle.*

We are not alone. We are not separate from God, from Spirit, from whatever you call the divine. We are all one. When we keep asking for the signals that show our oneness, it works. We can use it for the most mundane and basic things in our lives including prosperity, health, and relationships. Spirit is here to support us at every single level of our being.

SACRED GEOMETRY–SPACE/TIME CONTINUUM

Numbers, measurements, patterns, frequencies, cycles, angles, and time express energetic relationships throughout Universe.

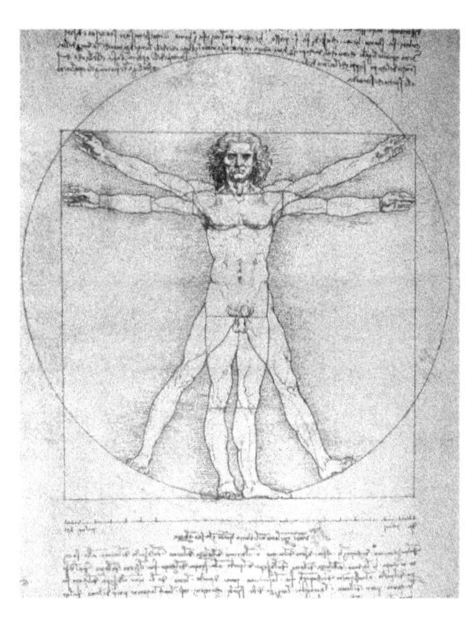

Source resonates with the physical and creates energetic relationships throughout the Universe and higher dimensions using:

number	measure
pattern	frequency
cycle	angle
time	

Sacred Geometry
Space/Time Continuum

Fig. 3-2

The Vitruvian Man by Leonardo da Vinci (Fig. 3-2) is a wonderful example displaying how the human body is built upon mathematical ratios that are found consistently throughout the animal and plant kingdoms. Source resonates with the way the body and all organic physical form is created through specific repetitive geometric ratios. These patterns are the fabric Source requires for its connection working with numbers, patterns, and the cycles of time. Energy flows often move in a spiral that is measured in frequencies of oscillation in Hertz which is impacted by the geometry and angles. These elements are crucial aspects of Sacred Geometry and can help us understand the vastness of our space-time continuum.

THE IMPORTANCE OF NUMBERS

Numbers are more than just a way to count quantities. We can assign them qualities and even genders to better understand the nature of the energies we are working with. (Fig. 3-3) Odd numbers are more masculine in nature. Numbers 1, 3, 5, and 7 are initiating, activating, energetic, and transformative. They can't be lined up in even rows because they can't pair, which is part of how they initiate and activate. Even numbers, which feel more feminine, will line up evenly, showing more balance and ability to work together. They're stable and receptive in their nature. Odd numbers work on what's in the field, while even numbers are the field. 2 – 4 – 6 – 8 hold the space for the work to be done.

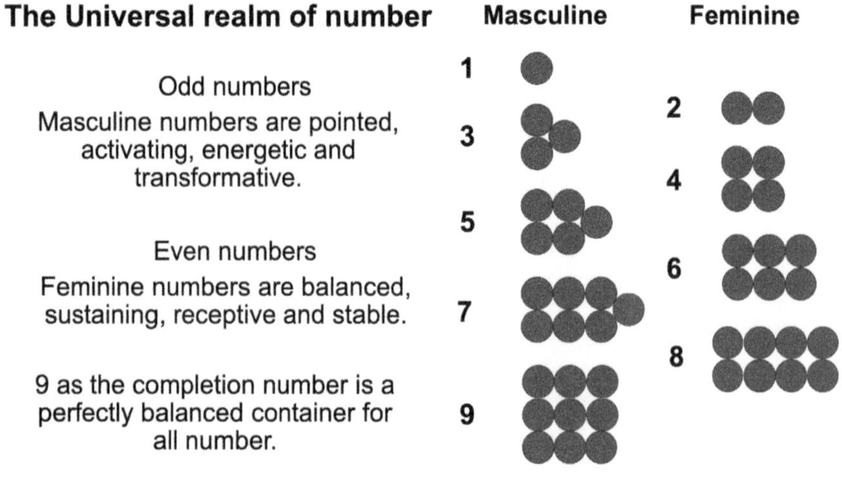

The Universal realm of number **Masculine** **Feminine**

Odd numbers
Masculine numbers are pointed, activating, energetic and transformative.

Even numbers
Feminine numbers are balanced, sustaining, receptive and stable.

9 as the completion number is a perfectly balanced container for all number.

1 3 5 7 9
2 4 6 8

Fig. 3-3

The masculine is the initiating and transformative principle. It's what gets the process moving. The feminine aspect is what's needed to ground and stabilize it. The masculine in and of itself would keep initiating and disrupting progress, leading to breakdown. It is the feminine aspect that keeps things growing, sustained, and connected.

The masculine principle initiates and transforms, but without the feminine grounding and stabilizing, nothing could remain in existence.

THE CIRCLE: SOURCE AT ITS CENTER

The *first element is shown by the circle.* The first impulse moves out equally in all directions the way a pebble dropped in still water creates concentric circles moving outward, always equidistant from its center. This is a perfect metaphor for the beginning symbol that stands for universal principles and a symbol for consciousness. The circle with a dot in the center reflects Source at the core with the potential of infinite expansion, remaining equidistant with the expanding edge of the outer circle. You can travel forever on its edge and always keep moving through time, becoming a spiral and evolving into a new level of understanding.

The circle with Source at its center symbolizes the highest aspect of creation.

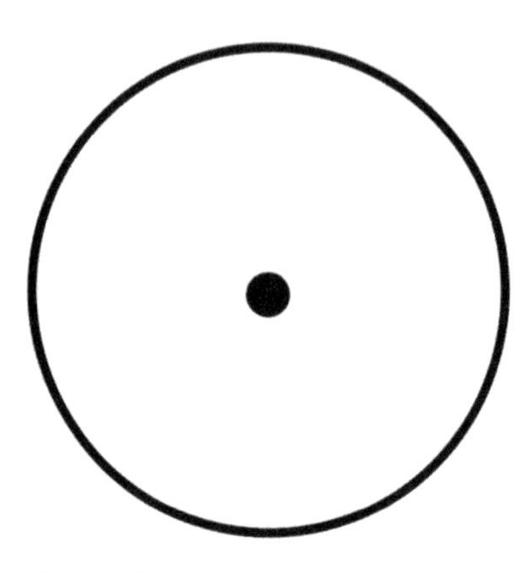

Fig. 3-4

Gaze at that large circle with the dot in the center (Fig. 3-4) and let it remind you of your soul within the larger embrace of that which is God and Unity.

The center dot is the Source. The circle with a center dot was understood by the Pythagoreans as the Monad, the initial, activating, creative source of everything. The circle is a symbol for unity, and with the dot in the middle, it becomes the all-seeing eye at the peak of the pyramid on every US dollar bill and in astrology, it's the symbol for the sun. The circle is used as a sign for God and for Soul. This refers to the highest aspect of creation that allows us to connect with source and the unified field.

We see it in the letters of our alphabet, where you have the circle shape for the letter O in the center of the words Monad, God, and Source. It isn't by accident that we have particular shapes for letters that create our words. (Fig. 3-5)

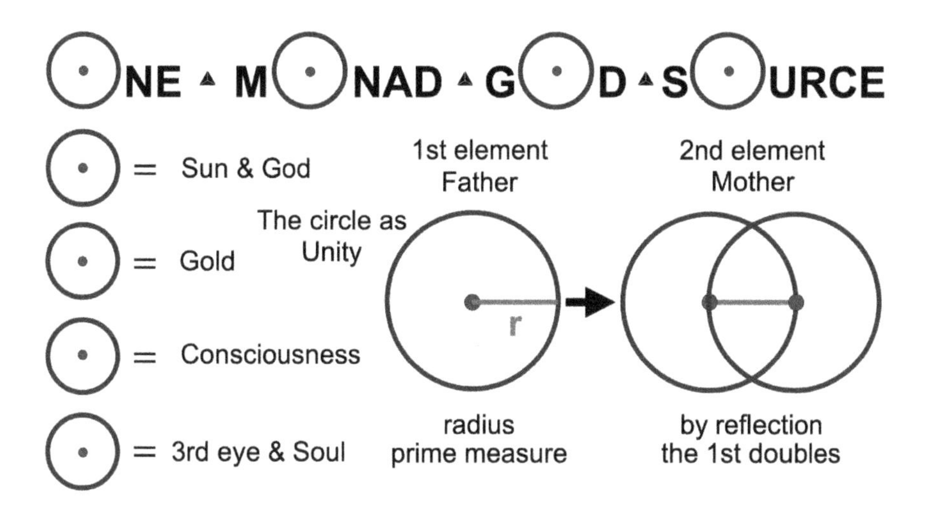

Fig. 3-5

The first element is masculine in nature: father. A measurement from the center to the edge of the circle is known as the radius. The radius carries all the information that you need to define the size of a circle or a three-dimensional sphere.

For consciousness to expand, change is introduced by the Monad. A perfect reflection is created that is an exact duplicate. A second circle that has the same radius moves out from the first circle. To maintain relationship and connection so energy can flow, the second circle has its radius overlap the first radius. This places the center of each circle on the edge of its reflection. This offers the second element which introduces the feminine aspect, a mirroring of the first Monad. This is reminiscent of the Adam and Eve story where the rib (supporting radius) is taken from Adam to create Eve. It separates unity into two equal individualized aspects.

NUMBER 1: THE ORIGIN OF ALL

The Monad/Source is the beginning and identified as the number 1. It's the divine aspect of everything that is found in unity and as such it's the universal divisor of all other numbers. Everything can be divided by one; it's the only number that can divide into every number. However, there's an issue with it. If you divide something by one, you get the same number again. **One exists within everything. Every single number contains 1 within it.** Source (1) exists within all of us, but it's very difficult to find. It's actually unknowable in many instances, in the mathematical world, in the way that other numbers can be known and worked with, for when you multiply one with another number, you will always get the same number again. Multiplying by one or dividing by one, you only see the surface, the other or outer component. Number 1 stays hidden and out of reach.

1 represents the divine aspect and is the universal divisor of all numbers.
9 ÷ 1 = 9. 1 exists within all but is unseen and unknowable.
Even multiplication (1 × 9 = 9) reverts to the original number.
The power of the first impulse (1) is hidden in our reality.

It is fascinating that 1 in and of itself doesn't go anywhere. In the physical dimension, energy must flow. Energy is catalytic and constantly changing things. However, 1 on its own is static. It's just there. In meditation, we breathe and relax to reach a still point, a blissful or peaceful state. That still point is something that attracts us to reach for, but we never fully get there. It's where nothing is happening and our mind and sensory perceptions are always working to explore and interact with the environment. Life gets interesting through the connections we make. The first primary human relationship is when a baby connects with its mother. Without its mother, the child will not survive. This demonstrates that 1 in and of itself is a divine beginning; however, we move out from that perfect beginning to explore a world that can sometimes be very interesting and challenging.

Number 1 seems to fade into the background and appears to wield so little power in our numerical world; however, it represents Source and the Unity that all of us are trying to rediscover. Number 1 is the power of the first impulse and the Divine Masculine hidden in our reality.

NUMBER 2: DUALITY, SEPARATION, CONTRAST

As we progress into the next number, we are shown that 2 becomes the doorway to the divine aspect of the feminine, which enables us to enter the physical world through the experience of duality. Number 2 is all about a world of separation and contrast. Duality can be looked at through the lens of good or evil, and we can see it as the mixing of the two elements, as shown in the yin- yang symbol (Fig. 3-6). The positive aspects of duality lead to recognition of the other. When Source originally separated and created dual aspects through its own reflection, you and I could begin to play and interact. There could not be a Mother and Child without duality and separation.

Number 2 becomes the doorway of the Divine Mother into the physical world. It is through duality that we recognize the other. With separation, energy can flow. With contrast, beauty and love can be discerned.

The baby who is in the womb safely developing until it is birthed is not fully alive yet. It's alive within the structure of the womb, but it has not taken its first breath and gone through the separation and transition into individualized life. The baby is born with the umbilical cord still intact until it's no longer functional. It is a critical point when the umbilical cord is cut and the full separation is achieved. As human beings experiencing duality, perhaps if we recognize the power of that transitional moment, we could grieve the loss of oneness and the perfect world of the womb that we've emerged from where everything is provided. We had all that was needed except life on its own.

When we are born, and the first breath is taken, the emotions are accessible. A baby cries in response to emerging into the outside world. It's the beginning of separation and that separation gives us life. Separation is blueprinted into us and is loaded with opportunity. And yet reconnecting to the Source of life is the master plan, not to be led primarily through the ego, which is our persona based on separation and focused on purely physical needs. Our life process is about incorporating every stage of growth to unite with the bigger part of who we are, discovering and rediscovering physical life from a greater perspective. By coming into connection, we realize this is our opportunity not to leave this place, but to incorporate something larger into our lives. Then it will be for the good of all and we can know what love truly is. We can touch upon infinity in our soul because we realize what it is, elevating consciousness for this life and the future. It's an amazing process to connect to the larger whole, healing the pain and dysfunction of separation.

Separation is blueprinted into us and is loaded with opportunity.

THE DANCE BETWEEN ONENESS AND DUALITY

Because of separation, energy can flow. All the energy in Universe needs to be active and moving. It can't remain static. When separation happens, there is a difference in polarity and potential so energy can flow from one place to another. Much of what creates energetic flow is resonance. When you resonate with something, you begin merging with that energy, which initiates the creation process. This is the dance with oneness and duality. The resonance aligns with certain energies you're visualizing and feeling. Separation and contrast allow us to discern things like beauty and love. Through the experience of what isn't love and what pain feels like, the emotions of sadness and guilt teach us what isn't sad, what isn't guilty. It's not meant for us to stay there forever, but to touch upon all these emotions to deepen the human-soul experience.

We live on a free-will planet with an abundance of choice and variation. In quantum physics, we can't discern reality without the recognition of an observer. All the contrasts make us aware of choices that enable us to rise to a certain resonance and vibrational level, to become active in that field of creation.

Duality, separation, and contrast are all part of what comes with number 2. The Father still remains unknowable, however 2 becomes the pathway from Source into the physical dimension and it is also the way back to Source. In Fig. 3-5 there are two circles showing the reflection of the 1, the Father with the Mother. Number 2 as the Divine Feminine is responsible for the initiation of our existence. She became the first step out from oneness into multiplicity and she remains the doorway for us to return to the higher realms and Source. This is the nature of 2. It is also why there is so much importance placed upon the feminine recently. The feminine has been suppressed for a very long time, which limits our ability to reach into the higher dimensions and Source. Part of overcoming the struggle between light and dark is returning to the balance between masculine and feminine.

> **Father (1) remains unknowable with the only pathway to/from Source being the doorway of the Divine Mother (2). The Mother (2) is responsible for the initiation of our existence and is the doorway back to Source.**

As the feminine comes back into balance, we can access the Father again and Source itself. We can't get there on our own or through domination of one over the other. The balance of all elements is necessary for the good of all.

As the flow opens, we have this dance between the initiating 1 and the manifesting 2, the male and the female, seeking balance. The intertwining caduceus coil and the DNA design represent how we move in and out of each other spiraling around a gravitational attraction of love. We're moving into this new epoch, where we're seeking balance so that creative flow can happen again. The status quo limits us by curtailing the dance and the energy movement. We need both, and the more we honor all the polarities, all the different aspects of what is here in our reality, the more we can embrace wholeness.

DUALITY: THE FLOW OF OPPOSITES

> **The two-sided snake with a forked tongue that interacted with Eve personifies the second principle of duality and separation.**

In much of Eastern thought, duality is seen as the intermingling flow of opposites and the resulting movement between them allows for transformation. The yin-yang symbol describes reality as made up of opposite but interconnected forces of creation.

At the center of darkness is a core of light, and in every bit of light there is found a small speck of darkness. That's why those opposing colors are there in these two movements, swimming in the circle, and the two circles in the center. (Fig. 3-6)

> **In Eastern thought, duality is seen as the intermingling flow of opposites to allow for transformation. A small part of the darkness is at the core of light and light is found within all darkness.**

Fig. 3-6

In the West we focus more on the polarity expressed in the Bible as irreconcilable opposites. In Genesis, this duality is focused on the knowledge of good and evil.

Adam and Eve are archetypes that stand for more than just characters in a biblical story. They're representing the roles of the masculine and the feminine. Eve is introducing us to the feminine principle. She shows us the duality that exists within knowledge as an expression of the spectrum of good and evil, which is what happens as we fall from the higher realms of the father. As the child is born, they leave the higher world of connection, enter the birth canal, and forget the knowledge of everything that happened before. This expunges what was earlier learned and engages the discovery process. The blank canvas to an artist is an exhilarating and challenging platform for creation.

The Mother offers life. When we leave the realms of the Father and the Spirit comes into matter, it enters through the Mother. To step into matter, we must go through Mother—the feminine principle. It is not by accident that the Latin word for mother is mater.

One of the most dualistic of characters is the snake. The two-sided snake also has a forked tongue and that's what interacted with Eve as the personification of the second principle, the knowledge of good and evil. A snake represents duality because of its nature and how it moves with its belly to the earth. The western interpretation of a snake is that it demonstrates separation in its very existence. However, there are many places around the world where, for thousands of years prior to Christianity, snakes had been seen as a positive symbol of wisdom.

In Egypt, wall carvings of snakes symbolized the transmission of higher wisdom and energy flow. In the Mayan culture, Quetzalcoatl was a god who displayed the form of a feathered serpent. Carvings of the meditating Buddha sometimes have an aura of seven snakes, representing the linking of his chakra system to the wisdom of higher realms. The enlightenment process of kundalini is seen as intertwined serpents raising earthbound energy back into a union with the Divine. In the medical staff, the intertwined serpents are establishing wisdom in medical practice.

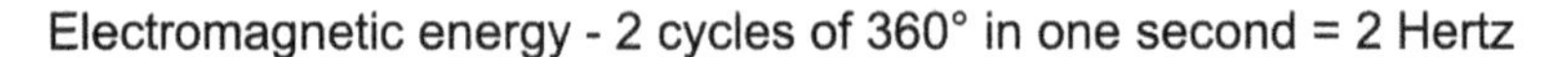

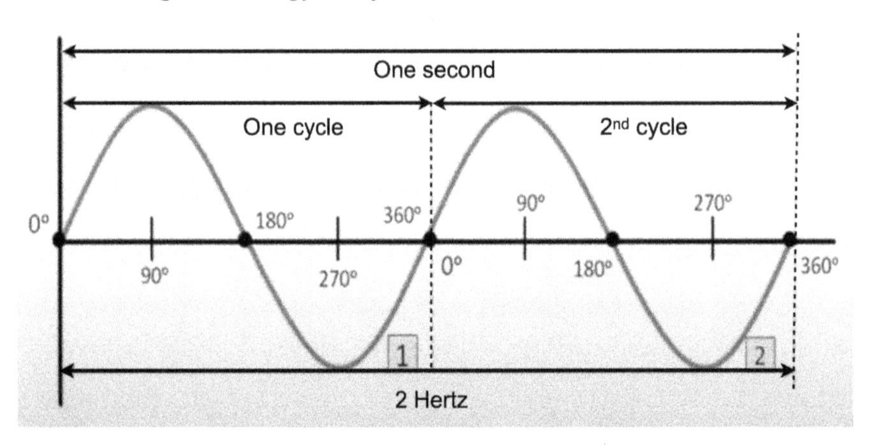

Fig. 3-7

It's important to note that the image of the undulating sine wave in Fig. 3-7 is not an accurate representation of the way energy moves. We are three-dimensional beings that almost exclusively use two-dimensional constructs to communicate. Books, computers, and smartphones all distort reality by forcing it into a flat, two-dimensional view. We translate in our minds all the images that we see in flatland books, but sometimes reality is grossly distorted, and we come to believe the distortion. The energetic vibration depicted above is actually a spiral in 3D. If the spiral is projected onto a flat surface from its side at a right angle, it does look like the undulating sine wave that we always see in books. In reality, waves of energy corkscrew through our world as spirals, and if we look at them head on, they are seen as perfect circles, which is where we started at the beginning of this chapter with the symbol for Source/God as the container of all.

> ***If you want to find the secrets of the universe, think in terms of energy, frequency, and vibration.***
>
> ***—Nikola Tesla***

This is one of Nikola Tesla's most famous quotations, and although it appears that he is speaking about several different things, it is truly only one thing: The way energy moves is through resonant harmonics. We all agree that everything is energy, and it is usually vibrating. A complete cycle of vibration as seen in Fig. 3-7 moves from one extreme high position to the other extreme low position and back again for a full cycle. The number of cycles that occur in one second is known as frequency and is measured in hertz (Hz). What Tesla was referencing is that everything (energy) vibrates, and to understand how it works with everything else can be understood through the numbers related to its frequency (rate of vibration).

Tesla was playing with this concept in 1898 with a vibrating device the size of an alarm clock. He attached it to a ten-story-high, half-built steel building in the Wall Street district of New York City. Within a short while, the structure began to tremble and then began creaking and weaving. He removed it before any real damage was done, but he boasted to the police and reporters who had arrived that, "He could just as easily destroy the Brooklyn Bridge in a matter of minutes if he felt like it."[4] He played with different frequencies, finding some that caused his office chairs to dance about while others created earthquakes in New York's Chinatown. When the right frequency for a physical object is found it is understood as its harmonic. This is what happens when a frequency for middle "C" is played on a piano and a tuning fork aligned with that same frequency will start to vibrate.

> **Harmonic resonance expands or contracts in whole numbers, only through Source numbers 1 and 2. 1 is Unity, and 2 is the doorway that swings into and out of Unity.**

After traveling through the first nine numbers, we return to 1 as 10, number 1 plus a placeholder we call zero as it has no intrinsic value. Number 10 has the original attributes of Source 1 in that it doesn't change the essence of any of the numbers that it multiplies or divides into, so each result is essentially the same number and thus is resonant with itself. What does change is the magnitude of the number. For example, the following numbers are vibrationally resonant with each other: 432 - 4,320 - 43,200 - 432,000. In essence, they are all the same vibration acting at different levels of force/power/magnitude.

---

4 Margaret Cheney, *Tesla: Man Out of Time* (New York: Touchstone, a division of Simon & Schuster, 2001) page 116.

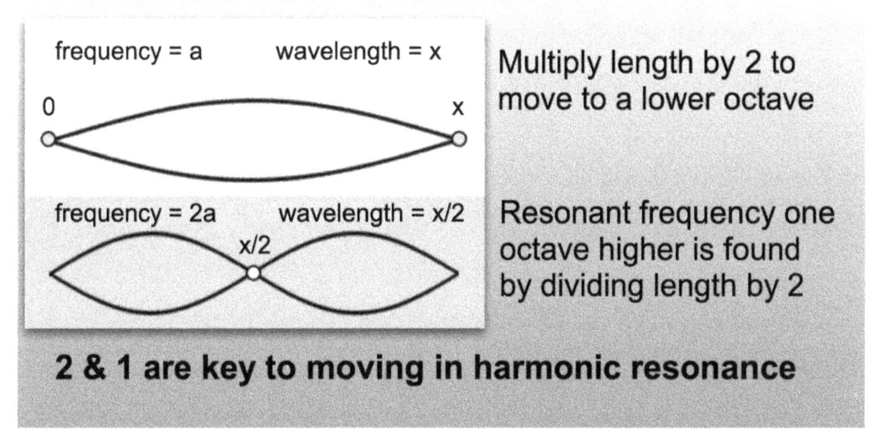

Fig. 3-8

Number 2 is the true change agent that allows numbers that appear as different to be harmonically resonant with each other. The proof of this was demonstrated over 2,500 years ago by a remarkable Greek sacred geometer known as Pythagoras (Fig. 3-8). What he shared was an understanding that a string of a certain length under tension produced a particular note when plucked. If that note was middle C and the string was cut in half (divided by 2), then the resulting note, also C, was resonant with the first, but one octave higher. If the string was doubled (x2) in length, then the resulting note was C one octave lower. These three notes are harmonically resonant with each other, which means that if one is plucked, the other two will vibrate sympathetically demonstrating harmonic resonance and energy transfer using 2 as the multiplier or divisor. Middle C (252 Hz) × 2 = higher octave C (504 Hz) or (252 Hz) / 2 = lower octave C (126 Hz). This understanding of multiplying or dividing by 2 to achieve harmonic resonance carries over into every aspect of creation.

We might think that there could be many possible harmonic progressions, but there are only two seed numbers of energetic significance using the progression of 2. Starting with the seed number of $1 \times 2 = 2 \times 2 = 4$, $4 \times 2 = 8$..., which leaves 3, 5, 6, 7, and 9 as unused numbers. The 5 progression: $5 \times 2 = 10$, $10 \times 2 = 20$ and $20 \times 2 = 40$... is the same as 1 with an added degree of magnitude (0). Number 6 appears as the doubling of 3, and 7 is the odd man out with no sacred numbers in this progression. 9 is another aspect of 3 found through $3^2 = 9$ ($3 \times 3 = 9$) 3 is the source and energetic seed of all sacred harmonics as we will discover in the next chapter.

TAKE A MOMENT TO REFLECT . . .

Relating to universal patterns at the core of Sacred Geometry is a doorway for connection. It welcomes us back to live a life where we remember within our Soul and feel at home on this planet. When we listen to the sounds of crickets and the songs of birds, we feel comfort and relationship with the earth. The rhythms touch a place within to restore balance and reach a higher chord of our humanity. Nature nurtures and helps us overcome the pain of separation. We all struggle with that loneliness at some level and at different times. Humans yearn to belong to a family, a community, a tribe, or group.

As we travel into new territory to raise our vibration and embrace unity, we can see and sensitively experience what created wounds of separation and broken trust with people in our life. Take a few deep breaths and allow the disconnections you felt to find a more peaceful state. Feel the opening in your heart as you breathe and invoke your intent to release these limiting beliefs. Let your Soul direct you.

This is an important time to renew the vows to who you truly are. Listen to the messages inside. If they bring you to a place of greater peace and happiness, they will lead you in a good direction. Connection is essential and can overcome the control of the ego mind. You are here for the good of all. Release judgment that has held you back. Judgment, shame, and fear are indications of disconnection from Soul. Learn to recognize those states as a message from your Soul to redirect and choose acceptance of your divine self.

Fill yourself with gratitude for your life, loved ones, and the joys that are available to you. Choose a gentle, compassionate, and loving path, one that includes generosity and prosperity. When you are connected, you are in the flow.

Take a breath and open your heart. Feel your place of belonging here and now. Understanding geometry and number works at the core level to bring us back in touch with soul and the Divine patterns of all that is, beyond time, space, and mind. The Universe is an amazing, abundant, and loving system that welcomes you fully. Embrace the deep connection you have to Universe and all souls on this planet. Allow the flow of energy to guide you and receive a deeper understanding of your connections to all life.

CHAPTER 4
THE THIRD ELEMENT CREATES EVERYTHING IN UNIVERSE

If you knew the magnificence of the 3, 6, and 9, you would have a key to the universe.

—Nikola Tesla

Nikola Tesla was a deeply intuitive individual who was able to invent things that no one had previously thought about, and his concepts worked because he understood certain core principles. His innovations with electricity, alternating current, wireless technologies, and concepts of free energy demonstrated his extraordinary understanding of the unseen world and curiosity about how Universe operated. Not as a machine, but an awesome energy-generating system following patterns, frequencies, and cycles.

We are builders and creators that can expand our abilities when we are in resonance with Universe and follow how energy creates physical matter. In many ancient temples and constructions, buildings were inspired by higher spiritual values, and they were built following the patterns of the natural world. Many of the creations built during modern times are devoid of these important relationships and limit our ability to be fully connected. Understanding universal basics or archetypes gives us the foundation to create in a more holistic, healthy, and expanded way for the future.

At the end of the previous chapter, we shared that number 3 is the energetic seed of all sacred harmonics, and it is much more. Ancient people used to count 1-me, 2-you, 3-everything else. This tells us that 3 carries the spark of creation originating within Source 1 into all of manifestation. Number 3 is also the seed that catalyzes action and transformation.

As much as it is important knowledge to understand how 6 and 9 interact with our world, they would not exist without 3. The nature of 3 creates both of them. Many of us plant tulip and iris bulbs in the fall. The leaves and flowers that grow from it the following spring fulfill important functions, but they would not exist without the bulb that came first. In fact, they both eventually fall away, leaving us again with the original bulb. In a similar way, 6 is composed of 3 + 3. We see this in the way nature deals with 6-petaled flowers. Look closely at the iris bloom in Fig. 4-1. It has 3 petals forming a triangle on the inside growth and 3 petals interspersed on the outside growth. In 6-petaled flowers, two triangles of three elements each create the whole pattern. Likewise, a 6-pointed star is made from one triangle pointing up overlaid by a second triangle pointing down. If you add a third triangle you have 9 points, which is the completion number created by 32 (3 squared = 3 × 3).

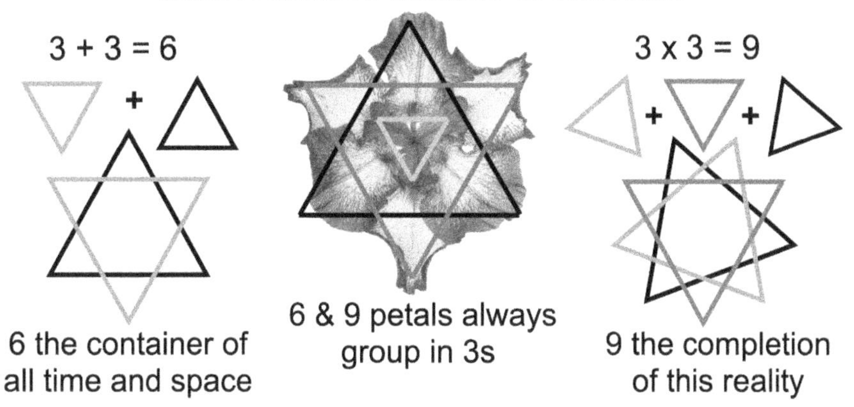

Fig. 4-1

The number 3 puts us in touch with the trilogy, the fulfillment of the creative process. It is the most active, generative, and transformative number in Universe. Ultimately all numbers reduce down to the original 9. Understanding the values and qualities of these numbers will help us know the energy we're bringing into our lives using each of the numbers.

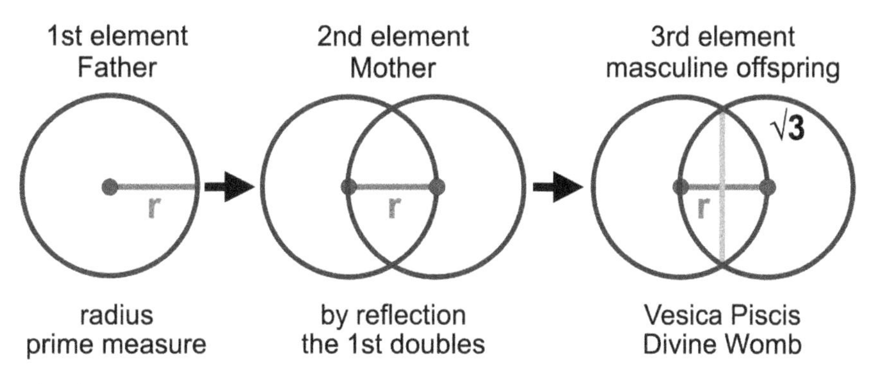

Fig. 4-2

Let's return to the model that we used before with Source symbolized as a circle. When it duplicates itself, so the second circle is one radius away, the edge of each circle overlaps the center of the other. They are joined in creating an almond shape in the space between them called a vesica piscis, which is Latin for "bladder of a fish." (Fig. 4-2)

From early times, this form was considered to be the divine womb because of its similarity to the female vulva, but more importantly, it's understood as giving birth to all of Sacred Geometry through the nature of its construction and the action of the divine feminine that brought it into existence. The image of the fish symbolized the Age of Pisces, which coincided with the birth of Christ. This coincidence with the age and the nature of the vesica piscis completing the trilogy of co-creation moved it into a prominent place in Christian symbology. Mother Mary and Jesus were often placed in the middle of a vesica piscis to reinforce their connection to holy principles.

THE ESSENCE OF CREATION

What this progression of numbers shows is the very essence of creation, with 1 being Father, and 2 being Mother—the balance of left/right brain and all polarities within us. Nothing is activated until they unite, which results in creation. We are the creation. We are also co-creators, working with the divine creative energy. Creativity is a fundamental quality of human life and everyone at some level exhibits creative expression, even though our culture and education has often suppressed the importance of developing that part of ourselves. The more we relate to ourselves as creative beings, the more we cultivate the natural ability to co-create. Creation is how we come together and evolve humanity. Ancient texts and icons show us explicit symbols and aspects of higher qualities of our humanity that we can achieve.

Many ancient cultures understood the deeper meanings embedded in number and form, which we often miss because we look at numbers merely as quantities, rather than representations of universal understanding. Their significance teaches us how to decode and utilize all these aspects in our lives.

From Divine Masculine, the Divine Mother creates this duality. However, she then creates the third element to birth the next level of creation, resolving duality through relationship. Within duality resides separation, with two components that don't seem to have anything visibly connecting them until a third element is introduced. Number 3 creates an interaction between two elements where there is dialogue or energy exchange between two aspects of creation, resulting in a third element that creates resonance or dissonance and change. Transformation happens because of 3, creating the momentum for change through the movement of energy and the basis of the relationship.

We grow through positive and negative relationships, which are key to our life journey. We only exist within relationship. Our existential struggle is the resolution of polarity through many different relationships, allowing us to grow by gaining insight and a deeper connection to the soul of humanity.

R. Buckminster Fuller showed us that every event in Universe has three parts - an action, reaction, and result. The momentum manifests the next action, reaction, and result. Fuller looked at Universe through this lens, seeing everything made up of threeness.

A triangle is the strongest, most stable of all the polygons. It's the only polygon that keeps its shape under pressure. A square, pentagon, or hexagon can be bent out of shape where the angles will shift, yet it's impossible to change the triangle, whether it's long, skinny, short, or fat. Each side supports the other two sides and it's impossible to shift the angles without breaking it.

The triangle adds structure for building because of its inherent strength. If we build with squares, it will eventually collapse. However, if we divide those squares into two triangles by adding a brace from one corner to the other, then we create structure and strength.

Triangles are also the best way to tile a plane or cover a complex three-dimensional surface. This is why computers use them in building graphic images and 3D engines deliver games where the fastest and simplest programing unfolds through triangulation.

Many of our most powerful concepts are expressed through the balanced display of the trilogy with each important component playing an equal part for greater strength and fullness of thought and expression. It is the perfect way for Source to be known as One through its attributes of truth, love, and beauty.

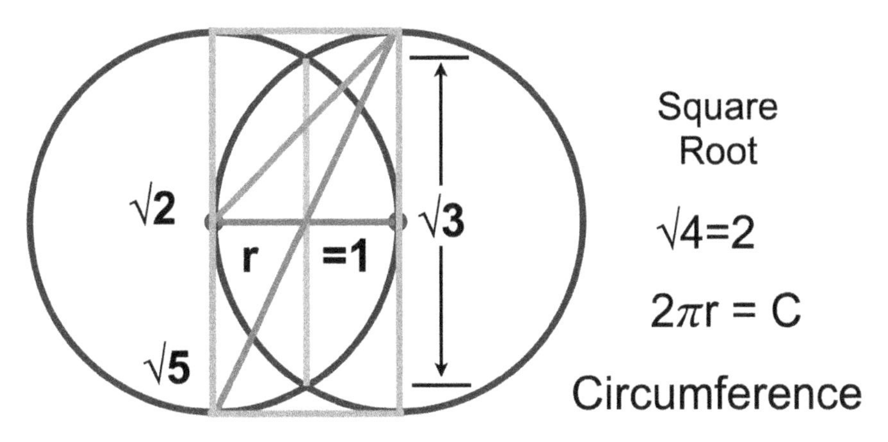

Fig. 4-3

THE GEOMETRY OF THE VESICA PISCIS OFFERS POTENTIAL

There are only four numerical relationships that are responsible for all the geometries in existence and each one is first unveiled in the overlapping circles we've been discussing.

First the radius itself creates a relationship with the circumference of the circle that offers the magical number of Pi (π – 3.141···), which is the ratio of the radius to the circumference of the circle. (Fig. 4-3) Next, we will discover the three essential roots of creation. The square root of a number is the factor that we can multiply by itself to get that number. The square root of 4 is 2 as $2 \times 2 = 4$.

If we give the radius a value of 1 (Unity) then the vertical line bisecting the almond shape of the vesica equals the square root of 3. I always love how Universe plays with these numbers as the third element has the height of the square root of 3 ($\sqrt{3}$ – 1.732···) and the proportion of the circle that it uses for one side of the fish bladder is one-third. We can draw a vertical line on both sides of the vesica extended to the edge of each circle. This creates a large rectangle cut in half by the radius to form two equal squares stacked within the rectangle. The diagonal of one of the squares is $\sqrt{2}$ (1.414···) and the diagonal of the large rectangle is $\sqrt{5}$ (2.236···). The remarkable thing is that only these four numerical ratios are used in building Universe. The Mother births through her divine womb all the ratios necessary for creation. The $\sqrt{2}$, the $\sqrt{3}$, the $\sqrt{5}$ and Pi (π).

Like the roots of a tree, the square roots of 2, 3, and 5 are essential for supporting the growth of all geometry. They are often invisible, as roots are, but the support is there as seen in the diagonal of a square = $\sqrt{2}$ and the height of two equilateral triangles divided by the base = $\sqrt{3}$. In his book on Sacred Geometry[5], Robert Lawlor shares that "the geometric root is an archetypal expression of the assimilative, generating, transformative function which is root."

Various roots display the qualities of different energetic flows. We can draw upon the unique quality of each root through the application of Sacred Geometry.

What is meant by this statement is that square roots of numbers have many important applications in mathematics, science, and engineering; however, in each of these cases, they are represented by intangible concepts. Numerically each of these roots and Pi are called infinite decimals or irrational numbers because they go on forever with an infinite string of numbers after the decimal point. The three dots at the end of each number represent this infinite progression. There is no resolution, no way

---

5 Lawlor, Robert. 1982. *Sacred Geometry:Philosophy and Practice*, Thames and Hudson Ltd., London

to embrace them as a complete expression, they are only mental concepts that are considered irrational and non-relatable.

These roots are called infinite decimals or irrational numbers because they go on forever, but in geometry, they can be perfectly reconciled.

$$\text{Pi } (\pi) = 3.1415926\cdots$$
$$\sqrt{2} = 1.4142135\cdots$$
$$\sqrt{3} = 1.7320508\cdots$$
$$\sqrt{5} = 2.2360679\cdots$$

Through Sacred Geometry, they can be expressed as physical constructs that are tangible, relatable, and physically resonant with the principles that created them. We witness this in their representation through the vesica piscis. We can draw each of these roots as physical lines of a certain proportion within a square, triangle, or rectangle. The roots are expressed in a definite, tangible, relatable manner. They are no longer imaginary or irrational. To raise them into resonance with our environment and our physical and subtle bodies, we need to lift them off the two-dimensional page and start constructing three-dimensional geometries with them.

With a three-dimensional, physical geometry, you have an opportunity to feel, see, and bring into your body the experience of these roots. That's what we've demonstrated with all the geometries we create. We've taken intangible, mental, Universal archetypes and made them into physical constructs that start to vibrate, just the way a C tuning fork, when it's properly made, will vibrate with a C tone. The geometries we create bring these abstract principles into physical reality so your body can experience it rather than remaining in the mental world of abstract thoughts. The geometries allow us to anchor these higher principles into the physical world.

This explains why people feel the various geometries we create and why they form energetic fields to support meditation, and healing work, and are a positive influence in our environment. They are liaisons to the energetic qualities of Universe. When we meditate under a beautiful form called the Merkaba of Oneness, we can connect at a much higher level because the geometries that we've created open us to work with that resonance. This allows us to come into a flow of energy and drink from that fountain, so we can experience universality, expand the value of our lives, and focus on what is joyful and loving. These roots spring into life throughout Sacred Geometry.

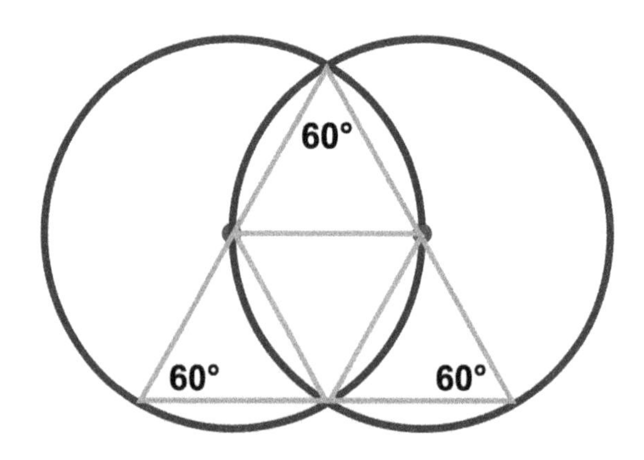

The 3rd element forms the 1st polygon a 3 sided triangle of 180°

The triangle is the measure of all polygons as each increases by 180°

Fig. 4-4

The power of the third element keeps expressing itself more and more as we discover that it also forms the first polygon, a three-sided triangle. A polygon is a geometry drawn on a flat plane that is made up of three or more straight lines. The number of degrees inside every triangle adds up to 180° regardless of its shape. Long or short, skinny, or fat, every polygon with three sides has interior angles that equal 180° and it becomes the base measure for all other polygons. In other words, if we add 180° to a triangle we get 360°, which are the number of degrees in the next polygon, a four-sided quadrilateral like a square, rectangle, or diamond shape. In this way, the vesica piscis leads us to all of the polygons. In addition, using only a compass and a straight edge we can construct all the polygons with the vesica as the seed geometry.

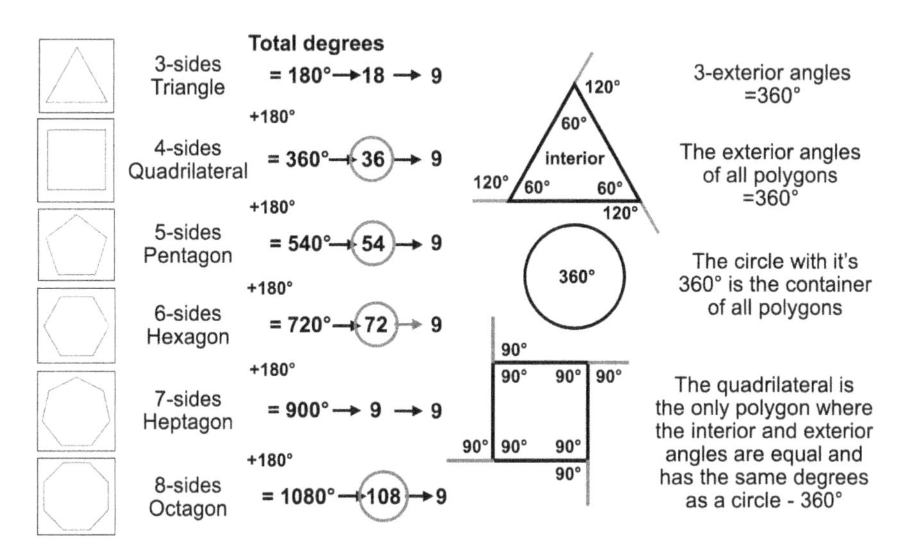

Fig. 4-5

As shown in Fig. 4-5, we can carry on with adding 180° to arrive at the next polygon with one additional side.

This progression will continue until the number of sides is indistinguishable from a circle. The threeness of the triangle with its 180° interior degrees is the unit of measure that steps us through all the other polygons. They all spring from the triangle, which gives birth to much more than we may have realized.

All the regular polygons fit within a circle where each point of the polygon rests on the circle's edge. Each polygon is contained by a circle of 360°. An interesting demonstration of the manner in which each polygon doubly displays this fact is found in their exterior angles. A straight line divides a circle in half and equals 180°. If we extend the edge of each polygon with a straight line, the exterior angle is 180° minus the interior angle. As you can see with the example of the triangle this formula gives us three angles of 120° (180° - 60° = 120°) for a total of 360° and so it continues for every polygon. The total of the exterior angles in every polygon equals 360°. Not only does each polygon fit within a circle, it also is surrounded in its exterior angles by the number of degrees contained by a circle – 360°.

ABSTRACT PATTERNS HAVE PRACTICAL APPLICATIONS

A practical application of this knowledge is demonstrated by the fact that a circle, understood as Source/Unity surrounds all 2D polygons, twice. What we have done at Metaforms with some of our jewelry pieces that are expressed in 2D is to put the 2D geometries within a circle, which creates a unity from the separate components, allowing the parts to act as a whole.

All the abstract concepts we are sharing have practical applications in our physical world. By building physical tools that incorporate the ways in which the higher dimensional realms express themselves, we can create resonant antenna systems that support the flow of higher dimensional energy into our environment. Many of these frequencies are needed for our health and well-being, however, as we've shared before, our present-day technology blocks these vital energies and sadly introduces many more toxic elements of its own.

If we look at the degrees in this ascending list of polygons a remarkable pattern unfolds. First, we can remove the zeros as we've learned that they don't change the root, only the magnitude. We now have a series of angles 36° - 54° - 72° - 108°. This series repeats indefinitely.

- 9-sides 1260° = 36° (add first two numbers)
- 10-sides 1,440° = 54°
- 11-sides 1,620° = 72°, and so on.

This series of numbers show up again and again in ancient sacred texts and is a pattern of consciousness instilling the universal design of life and awareness into every aspect of creation beginning with 3.

Another important pattern to recognize is that the total number of degrees in every polygon reduces to 9. When all the digits are added together, the total is 9. This is true for all geometric solids and all sacred numbers in sacred texts as well. It makes no difference what units of measure are used: degrees, miles, or years. In many texts the information is hidden as numbers of beads, fish, plants, or warriors. If it is an important sacred number it will reduce to 9, which is 3 squared. Number 9 is the completion number, the resonant container of Source factors. Resonance can occur between aspects of creation that appear separate such as time and space. 9 is an aspect of 3 that is completion. Number 3 starts the energy moving in the physical world, creating the diversity of form, and the squared aspect of 3 completes this reality through 9 as the container.

APPLYING WHAT WE'VE LEARNED FROM 3 AND 9

All the information we are sharing has greater purpose beyond the academic. One significant aspect of 3 is the relationship it triggers to take us beyond self and duality. The creative force, Spirit is embodied in everything, so consciously working with the quality of 3 allows us to embody unity and higher connections. Since our focus with the geometries we build is to enhance those higher connections, we've found that braiding three wires together that are then coiled creates a higher dimensional resonance past fourth-dimensional energy flows. Two twisted wires work with lower dimensional vibrations for physical healing and plant growth. When we wrap coils in our pendants and geometric forms we always use 9 wraps or a multiple of 9. Remember from the first chapter that energy moves in spirals? Reinforcing the natural movement of energy by constructing a spiral increases the flow by following a universal pattern. Nikola Tesla accomplished this in a similar way with his "Tesla Coils" for working with electricity. Constructing coils with 9 wraps or multiples of 9 creates the strongest energetic resonance with higher realms.

TAKE A MOMENT TO REFLECT . . .

We live in a Universe of infinite and dynamic creation that fills each moment with new life - all an offspring of Source. The imbued consciousness reflects magnificent patterns and purpose in the cycles of evolution. Our choice is to expand awareness and knowledge to meet each of these relationships with sincere appreciation.

As we find ourselves through the fragrance of a flower, the strength of a tree, or the joy of another human, we are offered a moment to experience divine relationship with all life.

Our physical senses speak to what is created, yet our higher non-physical senses lend love to the essence of all. The true gift of spirit.

Each moment is an opportunity to reclaim our connection by being fully present. As seen in the expanse of diversity, we have the freedom to build our lives, just as each flower, bird, or mineral evolves and grows in beauty. All united, yet distinctly individualized. When we are in the flow of creation, we thrive with gratitude.

CHAPTER 5
THE PATTERNS THAT GROUND REALITY

The first three numbers (1, 2, and 3) compose the Divine Trinity and form the invisible support for the growth of all of creation. The number 3 emerges as the initiating catalyst to set the next cycle in motion. The following three numbers (4, 5, and 6) are the structure that defines how our reality works. They define how resonant frequencies are created using these numbers as building blocks. By following their lead we can flow with creation by dancing in the same rhythms as Universe.

The number 4 is responsible for bringing us into the physical realm. We see this reflected in many of our metaphors as with the four corners of the world, the four directions, and the four physical elements of air, fire, water, and earth.

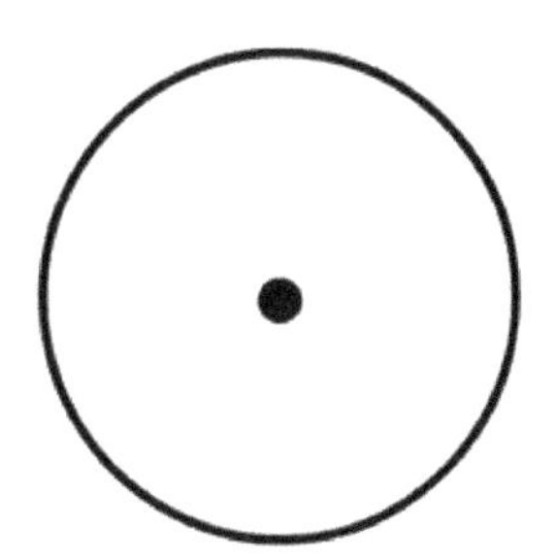

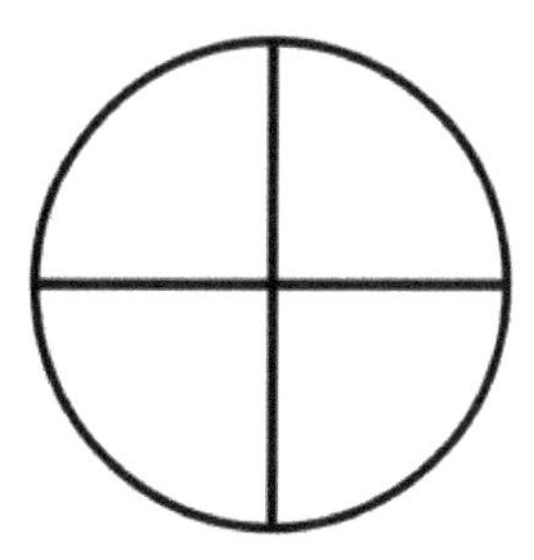

The circle with a dot in the center is recognized as the astrological symbol for the sun. The symbol for the Earth is a circle with a cross in the center neatly dividing it into four equal sections like the four seasons of a year. At the center of the cross are the four corners of 90° each, which points out a very curious relationship.

As we've already discussed, the circle is understood as Source, God, and the heavens above. The physical solid made of six squares, the cube, and the square itself have come to personify the earth and physicality. The two shapes couldn't be more different with one being made of a smooth infinite curve evoking feminine receptivity and the other having sharp angular corners seen as male assertiveness. Ancient sacred geometers tried to reconcile this difference by squaring the circle, which meant that they found mathematical and geometrical ways to create the same area inside a matched square and circle or they found a way to have the perimeters (the outside length) be equal. Degrees reflect the energy of where the shapes are found or used. The circle and the square are the quintessential display of "as above, so below." They appear to be so different, as far apart as heaven and earth, yet their essential overlap is understood by recognizing the 360° of the circle are equal to the 360° of the square. They are truly resonant and reflections of each other separated by outer perspectives. The similarities that exist escape our awareness if we only maintain the outside view.

This becomes a powerful metaphor to help understand that even though we look different on the outside, with all human beings having different features, skin colors, sizes, shapes, and belief systems, the internal resonance is what matters. The world gets caught up in the duality and separation principles of the binary 2 rather than working with the more evolved principles of resonance as demonstrated by the revelations of 4. The differences on the outside are not important when you look at the resonance that's created inside. Heaven and earth are resonant with each other when we understand this perspective and bring it into our lives. Everything can be resonant and connect when we dig deeply.

FROM DUALITY TO CO-CREATION

We are living in a time that is strongly focused on polarity. What if we viewed life as a progression from duality into co-creation, recognizing the higher values of what Universe really is and who we are? This way we shift our perspective in how we see things and perceive our lives. Computer technology influences all our lives very dramatically, as well as massive information gathering and expanding artificial intelligence (AI). Computer systems are based on a binary system of one and two, black and white, yes and no. Isn't that a reflection of what we see right now in our world? It seems more and more difficult to accept all the differences and wonderful gradients into the circle of possibilities. Instead, we tend to be focused on the polarity and separation that keeps the forces of duality in power.

Now, scientists are developing quantum computers and a higher computation capability that goes beyond the binary system and works within a quantum world of potential that more clearly aligns with the natural world. We may begin to leave behind the limitations of duality and polarity and progress to creating new ways of coming together that align with the natural order of universal principles. The more people understand universal secrets and the magnificence of creation in this way, the more empowered they become to move civilization onto a path of wholeness.

If we get stuck at the number 2 with its duality and separation it's impossible for us to evolve. We need to interact with all aspects of this reality and see its reflection within us as well. These numbers show us a natural path and a cycle of evolution to grow and become fully human.

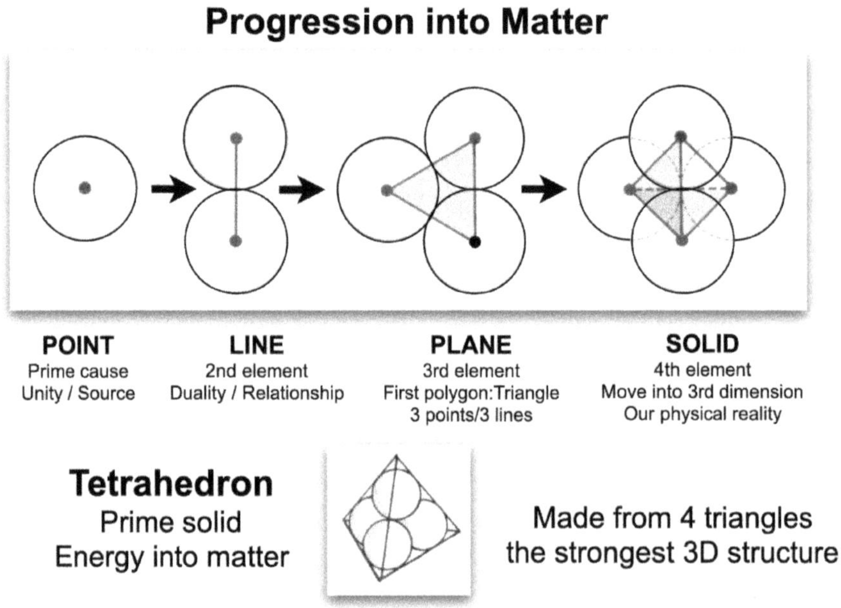

Progression into Matter

POINT
Prime cause
Unity / Source

LINE
2nd element
Duality / Relationship

PLANE
3rd element
First polygon:Triangle
3 points/3 lines

SOLID
4th element
Move into 3rd dimension
Our physical reality

Tetrahedron
Prime solid
Energy into matter

Made from 4 triangles
the strongest 3D structure

Fig. 5-1

If we look at the progression into matter (Fig. 5-1), first, we have the single point, which is the prime cause, Unity, and Source. Adding a second element creates a line between them, which is duality. By bringing in a third element, a plane is created. The simplest elemental plane formed by three points is a triangle, which is the first polygon with three points and three sides. The number 3 also has the potential of adding the third element to duality, creating relationship. When you take the first three elements and add a fourth element to them, you get the first solid form. This can most easily be visualized with small balls. Imagine holding three together to form a triangle and then add the fourth ball into the dip in the center. The fourth element/ ball moves the geometry from a plane/flat polygon into a three- dimensional solid. Laying straight rods against the outside of the balls reveals the first geometrical solid known as a *tetrahedron*, which is Greek for a "form with four sides." It has four triangular faces, four points, and six edges.

The tetrahedron is the prime solid. It's the first geometry we get in 3D reality. This shows that fourness gives us physical reality. The Greeks saw it as symbolizing the element of fire, which is appropriate considering that it is the first physical element that is transducing higher energy into the physical realm. It is indeed fiery and catalytic, too much so to be used by itself as a pyramid to meditate within. *Pyramid* was another Greek word that was used to describe the tetrahedron. It means "fire at the center," which is where the energy collected by the triangular faces is focused. It's also the strongest three-dimensional structure known, because each one of its faces is a triangle which is the strongest polygon with three faces focused around each point. A diamond is one of the hardest substances known, because its molecular structure of carbon atoms is made up of closely packed tetrahedrons.

> *The tetrahedron is the lowest common rational denominator of Universe.*
>
> *—R. Buckminster Fuller, Synergetics*

This is a very profound statement by R. Buckminster Fuller, the architectural genius and inventor of the geodesic dome. He understood structure and that the tetrahedron is the seed from which all other geometries grow. The first step into the physical is made by the feminine aspect of 4, which not only births this reality, but is also the catalyzing shape for the growth of all other geometries.

Only five three-dimensional geometries exist that have all faces that are identical in size, shape, angles, and edge lengths. They're called the platonic solids after the Greek philosopher Plato, who used them as descriptive elements in his well-known dialogue on the formation of Universe, *Timaeus*, written in 360 BC. Remember in the last chapter how the triangle with its 180 internal degrees became the measure for all the other 2D polygons? 180° triangle + 180° = 360° square + 180° = 540° pentagon and so forth. This assumes that all of the polygons have their points (vertices) touching the edge of a circle, and since the circle represents Source/God, we are discussing the polygons held by Unity. They follow the pattern of increasing in the rhythm of the 180° triangle that eventually as the number of sides increase returns to the circle/Unity.

The tetrahedron with its four triangular sides of 180° each equal 720° total (Fig. 5-2). It plays a similar role as the triangle, however, within the three-dimensional world. The sphere is the three-dimensional version of the circle where all the points of the solids touch the edge of a sphere/unity. When we add 720° to the tetrahedron, we get the next platonic solid called the octahedron with 1440°. To the Greeks, it symbolized air with its transitional qualities and movement. The cube at 2160° is the next form with its relationship to earth and the physical.

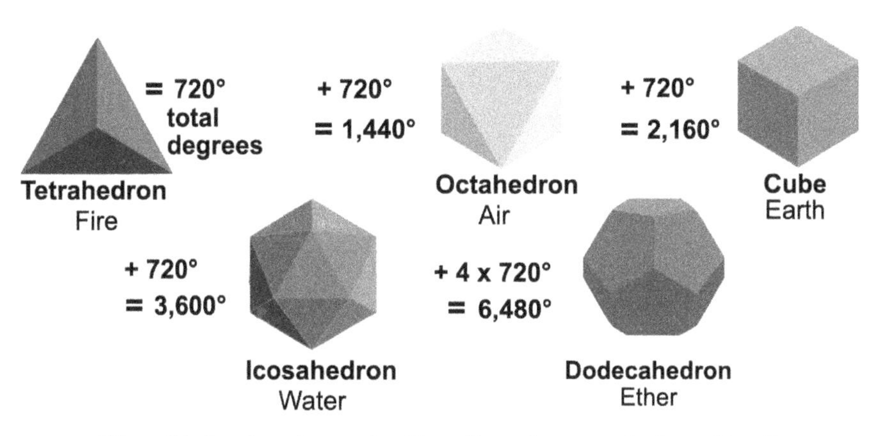

Fig. 5-2

The fourth wave of 720° creates the 20-sided icosahedron with triangular faces, and as the symbol for water, it bridges between the physical and non-physical. It vibrates with Soul and higher dimensions. An important clue about the icosahedron's ability to connect between heaven and earth is shown in its number of degrees: 3600°. This is resonant with the 360° of heaven's circle and the 360° of earth's square. This nature of water is the reason that a shower cleans more than your body—its movement also cleanses the energetic, etheric body that lies within a few inches of the physical.

The Japanese scientist Dr. Masaru Emoto researched how positive intent could be held by water to transform its purity. Water vibrationally enhanced by positive thoughts created more beautiful and perfectly formed snowflakes. In this case the perfection of the geometry as witnessed in the snowflake reflected the perfection of the thought.

Consciousness Affects Geometry and Vice Versa

This leads to the understanding that consciousness can affect geometry, and the reverse of this also holds true. When we are surrounded by perfect geometries made of the right materials we can be positively influenced as well. It is similar to how we feel when we are in a beautiful peaceful place in nature that reduces stress, enhances creativity, and promotes a feeling of connection that positively affects our health and well- being. Hundreds of research studies are now providing evidence for what we have known intuitively for so long. Spending time in nature improves our mental and physical health both in the long and short term.

Adding an additional 4 X 720° will take us to the final platonic solid, the dodecahedron, which symbolizes the non-physical, higher vibrational element of ether. Constructed of 12 pentagons, the dodecahedron binds life to the cosmological order of Universe. The component parts of the 5-pointed stars (see Fig. 6-5) formed on each of its faces, when the corners are connected by straight lines through the center, give us the phi ratio (1.618033···). This ratio is found by dividing the small parts of the star pentagram into the larger parts. It is a pattern present in all life from plants, insects and animals to human beings and the structure of our DNA. The number of its 12 faces embody "universal order and harmony" as described by the wonderful sacred geometer John Michell in his book *How the World Is Made*.[6]

The tetrahedron is not only the denominator of the five platonic solids, but it also evenly divides into every geometry that exists within a sphere including the 13 Archimedean solids. However, it goes still deeper into universal measures, as R. Buckminster Fuller suggested.

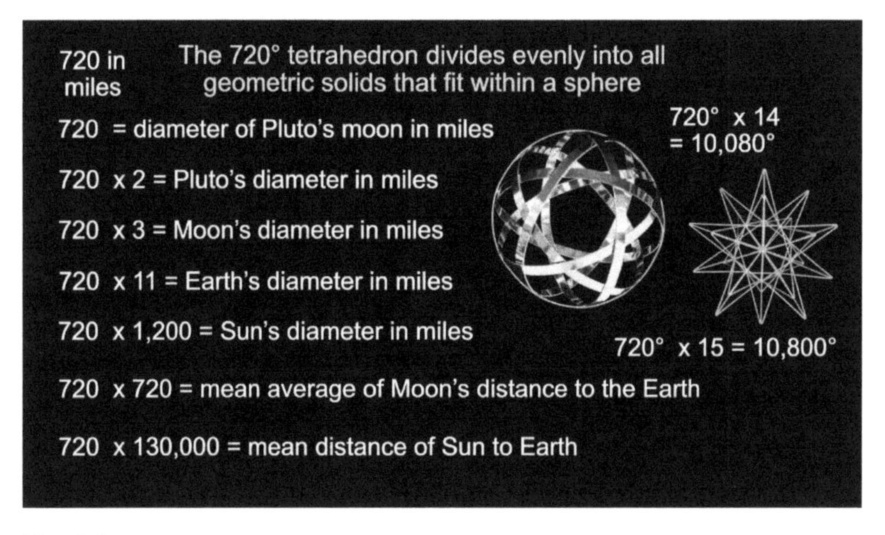

Fig. 5-3

6 John Michell, *How the World Is Made: The Story of Creation According to Sacred Geometry* (Rochester, VT: Inner Traditions, 2009).

The list of planets and distances exhibiting multiples of 720 miles, as seen in Fig. 5-3 poses the question: We were talking about degrees and 3D geometries and have now switched to miles, what is happening here? We were seeing how 720° was the common denominator for all these geometries and now we have brought in a list based on increments of 720 miles that shows us even divisions of the diameters of the Earth, moon, and more. In Eastern religions and metaphysics, people talk about the belief that "everything is connected" and "we are all one." Even in the field of quantum mechanics, we are discovering that the concept of quantum entanglement (inter-connectedness) is encompassing larger and larger swaths of reality. In Sacred Geometry, we watch numbers behave in certain patterns that replicate across different mediums connecting them in a similar resonance. In this case the importance of 720 as a rhythm or wave of energy is evidenced in geometry as degrees and in the physical Universe as a measure of distance or proportion quantifying celestial events among others. Celestial bodies such as our sun and planets act as intermediate waveguides for transducing archetypal energy to affect humans and planetary life.

SPACE AND TIME

When Albert Einstein was developing his theories on relativity, he concluded that space and time were not separate, unrelated phenomena. They are interwoven into a single continuum (called space-time) that spans multiple dimensions. What we are sharing now is that our geometer's space-time continuum expresses numerically harmonic connections between the degrees of geometry, the measure of space and the flow of time. A harmonic example of how time relates to 720 is seen when we convert it into minutes. 720 minutes are equal to 12 hours or half a day, which is a day or night cycle at the equator of planet earth.

Time is an expression of cycle and a function of rotation. The rotational speed of the earth gives us 24 hours in a day and its orbit around the sun offers the cycles of the seasons. We've found that spinning geometries at an appropriate rotational speed expands their energetic field and increases their fullness of expression by drawing in higher dimensional energy flows. The proper rotational speeds also reinforce important harmonics with time. Returning to our energy nodule of 720, we find that viewing it as hours gives us 30 days. The perfect month creates a year of 360 days. Most ancient cultures from the Mayans and Egyptians to the Sumerians observed a sacred year of 360 days. They considered the remaining five days to arrive at 365 to be unlucky and a time to retreat from the world. The sacred year is still with us today hidden within the Gregorian calendar.

In ancient Rome, December 25th was the pagan holiday of Saturnalia, a time of festivities and gift-giving. In 336 AD, it was designated by the newly formed Christian church to become the birthday of Jesus Christ. The regularity of the months has been manipulated many times in the distant past. Most notably by Julius and Augustus Caesar as they took days from February to make their months of July and August longer. On leap years, when February is given back one of its days, you can ask an information program what day is number 360, and it will come up as December 25th, the end of the sacred year of 360 days. Furthermore, remember the resonance of the divine circle of

360° with the square of Earth at 360°? When we work with a sacred year of 360 days, we expand and lock in that resonance through the cycle of time.

Now that the number 4 has opened the world of three dimensions, we are going to share how we create geometries that are resonant with these concepts. The Bible refers to "the four corners of the world," and we saw how that phrase possibly grew from the astrological symbol for earth where a circle is divided into four pieces like a quartered pie.

Many ancient cultures, from the builders of Stonehenge to Egyptian temples, oriented their structures around the rising sun. These events occurred at four equal intervals during a year: the winter and summer solstice for the shortest and longest days of the year with the two equinoxes in between when the balance between night and day are equal. It was the sunrise or sunset at each of these times that the ancients observed with their structures. Cycles of time move like circles through the heavens. Envision each corner of the square in the heavens as supporting a great circle, which is the largest circle that can be drawn around a sphere. Equally distribute these four equators or great circles, and a form of six squares and eight triangles is created (Fig. 5-4). These faces reflect the cube and the octahedron that have intertwined to create this geometry called a cuboctahedron. Bucky Fuller worked extensively with this geometry in the 1940s, referring to it as a "vector equilibrium" and "jitterbug" among other names. Its projection onto a sphere, as seen here, was researched in the 1950s by Dr. Derald Langham, an agricultural geneticist. He called it a Genesa crystal, a term that he also used to refer to all the platonic solids. He worked with large, curved structures where people stood inside and traced the circles with their arms to achieve better health and well-being.

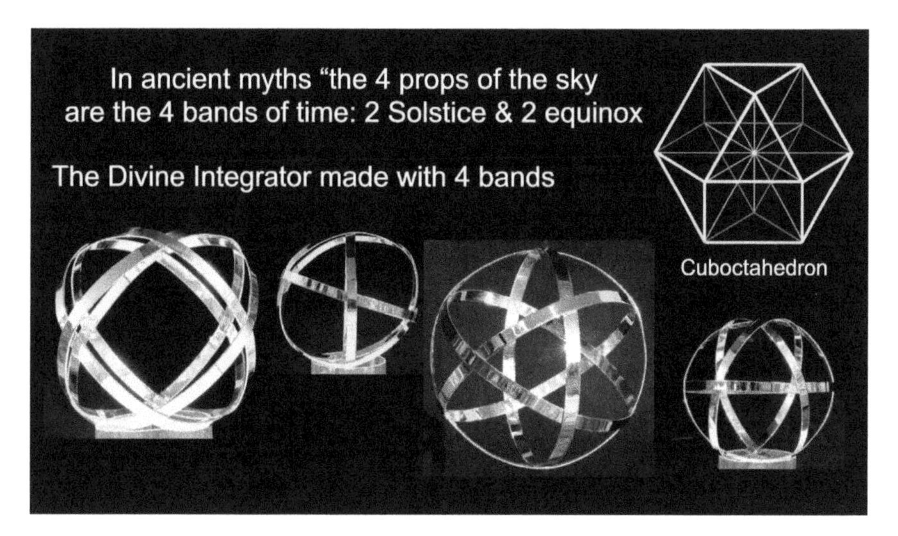

Fig. 5-4

We descriptively call it a Divine Integrator, for among other attributes, its total number of degrees is 3600°. Again, a form resonant with heaven, earth and the sacred year equaling 360. We spin or hang it with the axis passing through the cross as seen in Fig. 5-4. The Divine Integrator works with the seed Universal structure of time and space. It cleanses, balances, and amplifies higher vibrational energy for aligning the physical body with the spiritual body, connecting you to your divine essence of love.

This form creates a toroidal flow of cleansing energy that raises the frequency of the environment. It helps facilitate deep meditation, alignment, and intuition. You can use it to manifest what has not yet materialized in your life.

A Little Story from Gregory

I would like to share an experience that takes the power of following nature's example to a deeper level of feeling. I was on a canoe trip in Colorado at the end of a very warm day when a group of us decided to float the river in our life vests. Although the river was only waist deep, the bottom was difficult to walk on because of the many rounded stones moving with each step and a very swift current that was roaring against us. We formed a line moving toward the center. It was challenging to stay upright, and the noise of the water rushing past us made communication difficult. When we finally decided to drop into the flow, everything shifted. First was the quiet; flowing in the current with no disruption was so peaceful. The difficulties and struggle were gone as we effortlessly floated past the colorful scenery. Life's struggles and difficulties are often the result of going against the natural flow and order of life. We feel that we can conquer nature and impose our will, our needs. That day of floating impressed upon me the value and joy of going with the flow. Being propelled forward by sinking into what is, the power and support of accepting the natural order of Universe. When we relax into nature, we can feel the order within, and our body recognizes it deeply. It is our intent to replicate these same energies by constructing antenna systems following the patterns of creation.

TAKE A MOMENT TO REFLECT . . .

We've been exploring how the energy underlying everything creates harmonic resonance. Where there is resonance, energy flows and transformation can occur. In our work with sacred geometric technology, we have found that combining the harmonics of geometry, measure, and time in a single tool achieves the strongest energetic flow. Energy found in multiple expressions is overlaid and combined into one rhythmic dance, like the understanding of playing a single note versus a full chord. We use these numbers and their harmonics in the geometries and tools we create. We also work with various frequencies and certain types of geometries. We look at degrees in that geometry and we reduce it to see the expression of number we have, then we have a better understanding of the energy that geometry is giving us. It's all part of the grand scheme of creating resonance with life-positive, natural frequencies to vibrate our bodies by bringing these geometries into our sphere. They shift the frequencies of our environment, promoting the opposite effect of what computers and modern technology create that negatively affect our lives. We cannot block or erase their effects, but it is possible to restore balancing and higher vibrational energies to re-establish the expanded connections that have been lost.

CHAPTER 6
5 AT THE CENTER OF LIFE

There is an extraordinary order and pattern that intertwines all of Universe. As we watch the different cycles, patterns, and numbers come together and overlap, what appears to be the common focus from each unique direction is the creation and support of life. Life grows, evolves, and becomes more capable of embodying greater consciousness with the direction toward Unity, Love, Beauty, and Truth. In the end, all of creation springs from consciousness with the purpose of infinitely growing this seed.

We are central to this experience of expanding consciousness, although many people feel they're at the mercy of what's going on in their lives. They fail to recognize they are at the center of Universe connected to this consciousness and don't need to control events. As divine co-creators, we have a significant role to play. The intention and energy we hold in relationships and all circumstances we are involved with significantly affects what will happen. People who have meditated together in areas of turmoil and focused on peace for a particular city or a country have positively altered the energy and the course of events that was taking place. That meditative energy made a difference without people in those locations being aware that anything different was happening. The energy component was in play because everything is energy, and when we step into our higher divine aspect then we realize the evolutionary path we're on affects universal evolution. As co-creators of this Universe, we can align with all the universal patterns and precision of creation. The rhythm, cycles, and the exactness of the way Universe operates shows us who we are. In our everyday lives, we often forget that we are the center. However, when we return to resonating with many of these universal principles and secrets, we step into our role as divine co-creators and feel empowered. Notice the shift you feel within when you consider changing your perspective in this way.

AN ANCIENT STORY

The story had been passed through the records of ancient Egypt for thousands of years before the priests of a temple in the Nile Delta shared it with the Greek lawmaker Solon. That was in 600 BC, over a hundred years before it was passed down to Plato, who brought the story of the lost civilization of Atlantis to popular awareness. An advanced civilization was destroyed by floods and earthquakes in a single night over 11,600 years ago from our present time. The myths of ancient flooding can be found on every continent and in almost every sacred text, but until recently, that's all they were thought to be—myths. In the last couple of decades, scientists have been piecing together evidence of massive comet fragments hitting earth's thick northern ice sheets in approximately 10,800 BC and 9,600 BC. With the second strike, earth's oceans rose over 300 feet, destroying all coastal settlements and low-lying islands.

The evidence of this catastrophe being the death knell of an advanced civilization coincides with the overnight transformation of the world's hunter-gatherers into farmers and builders. This was a time of radical transformation. Many of earth's largest animals went extinct, and hundreds of new fruits, vegetables, grains, and domesticated animals suddenly appeared all over the world with the understanding of how to utilize and work with them. Calendars became very sophisticated with some like the Mayan calendar, made popular by its end date in 2012, accurately covering cycles of time over 26,000 years long.

This fascinating understanding of survivors of a prediluvian civilization passing on vital knowledge after an earth-changing catastrophe has been well researched and brilliantly presented by Graham Hancock in his two books, *Fingerprints of the Gods* and *Magicians of the Gods*.[7] Some of the information he draws upon for proof of survivors of an advanced civilization imparting their knowledge lies in a small list of sacred numbers that reveal themselves again and again throughout world cultures and religions. He correlates this list of numbers with measures of time. We agree with his correlations as we will share, however there is much more to decipher here.

As we stated in the last chapter, 720 aligns with time, measure, and degrees. When numbers transform into degrees,

---

7 Graham Hancock, *Fingerprints of the Gods* (New York: Three Rivers Press, 1995) and *Magicians of the Gods* (New York: St. Martin's Press, 2015).

we can have 3D geometries with the potential to act as antenna systems vibrating with the archetypal energy with which we can interact. What we are going to discover in this chapter are an expanded understanding of these sacred numbers gifted to us through time and how they spring from number 5.

THE NUMBER 5 IS AT THE CENTER

Number 5 is at the center of this focus on life; even numerically with the numbers 1-9, there are four numbers in front and four numbers behind 5. Universe likes balance and is using 5 as the center of the spiral of life.

Fig. 6-1

Life is miraculous and found everywhere on our planet—from microscopic bacteria and insects, to plants, animals, and humans. Despite the incredible variety of life, there is a common pattern we all share that is found in a ratio that has been observed for thousands of years. The Greeks designated it with their letter phi, **Φ**, and fashioned temples and statues following its proportions because they considered it a measure of beauty. From another perspective, perhaps beauty is what we see most frequently in the way nature expresses herself and what doesn't fit the usual pattern is considered to lack beauty. The phi proportion is frequently found as an expression of life, which is beautifully shown in the images in Fig. 6-1. The inherent nature of these patterns comes about because phi grows and spirals like the spiraling waves of light underlying reality.

Mathematically, phi can be found in several ways. As seen in Fig. 6-2, the square root of 5 (√5) is added to 1 and divided by 2 = 1.6180339··· = **Φ**. The three dots following this number mean that it has nonrepeating digits that go on forever to the right of the decimal point. It never ends, and thus, mathematicians consider it irrational in the sense that it never resolves or can be expressed as fraction.

$$\frac{\sqrt{5}+1}{2} = 1.6180339\cdots \quad \Phi$$

Fibonacci numbers

0,1,1,2,3,5,8,13,21,34,55,
89,144,233,377···

$$\frac{377}{233} = 1.618025\cdots \quad \Phi$$

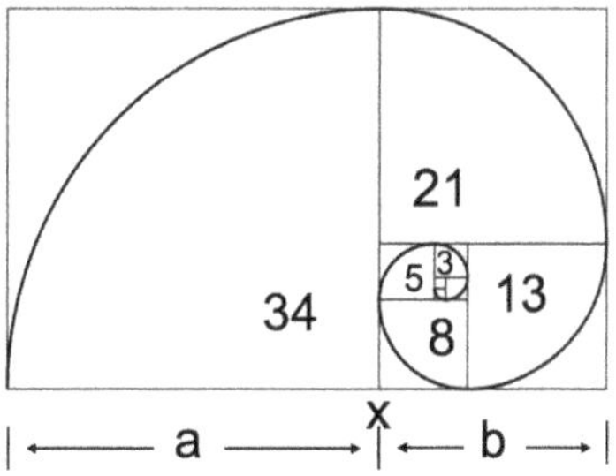

21
5 3
34 13
8
a x b

$$\frac{a}{b} = \frac{a+b}{a} = \Phi$$

Universe loves simplicity
Doing the most with the least

Fig. 6-2

Another way it can be calculated is by using the Fibonacci sequence. This is a series of numbers where each number is the sum of the two preceding numbers. The higher you go in this sequence, the closer you get to an exact expression of phi as shown in Fig. 6-2, the spiral formed on the right side grows with the side length of each square being the next number in the Fibonacci sequence.

We can understand the miracle of phi by looking at the line beneath the spiral with a large part (a) and a smaller part (b). The line is divided at the only point possible (x) where the small part (b) is divided into the large part (a) to give us a value of phi, **Φ**,1.6180339··· If you add (a+b) to equal the whole line and divide the total by (a) the larger part of the line, you also get **Φ** (1.6180339···). The side of each square growing the spiral is increasing in length by **Φ** over the previous square. Each square shows us a quarter of a circle drawn from one corner to the corner opposite it, but when the circle fragments are placed next to each other they grow in this special **Φ** spiral.

Another way of stating the relationship of the phi ratio line parts in Fig. 6-2 is: (b) is to (a) as (a) is to (b+a) In mathematical terms = (b:a::a:b+a). In describing relationships, we usually introduce a third element where we state that (b) is to (a) as (a) is to (c), but in this case with phi we've described a complicated set of relationships with only two elements, (a) and (b). Universe loves simplicity. This is doing the most with the least. It is true conservation of energy and something to emulate.

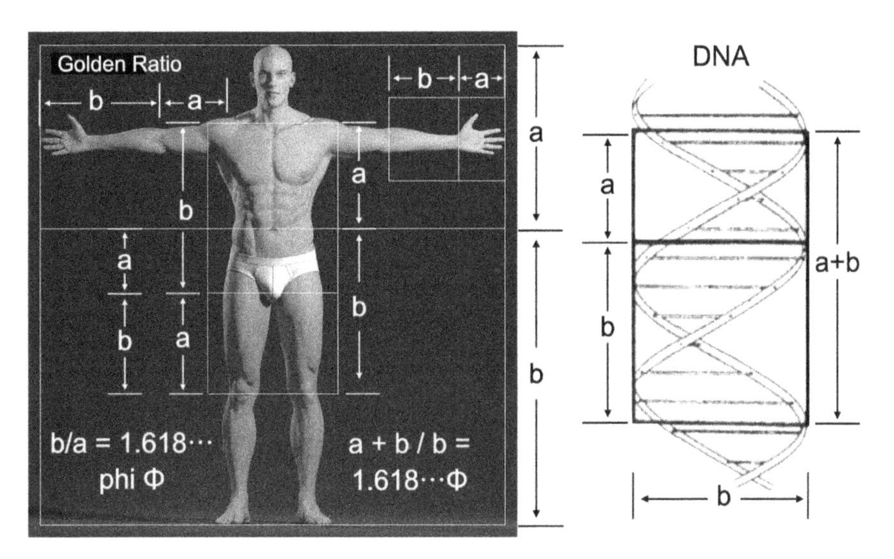

Fig. 6-3

Entire books have been dedicated to demonstrating how the phi relationship is seen in all aspects of life. In Fig. 6-3, we see how the human body demonstrates phi relationships. The shoulder to the elbow multiplied by phi (1.618···) takes us to the fingertips of the outstretched hand. The phi ratio is found by comparing the first digit to the whole finger of the middle finger and then the whole finger to the wrist and the whole hand to the elbow. The head to the navel times phi equals the distance to the feet. The averages of many human bodies continue to give us the same phi relationships. Even our DNA is an expression of this important relationship. Plastic surgeons rely on phi relationships to reconstruct faces we find beautiful. In this case, as we shared before, our judgement of beauty may simply arise from a recognition of what is most often found. What is different or unusual may wear the description of ugly.

RELATIONSHIP IS THE CORNERSTONE

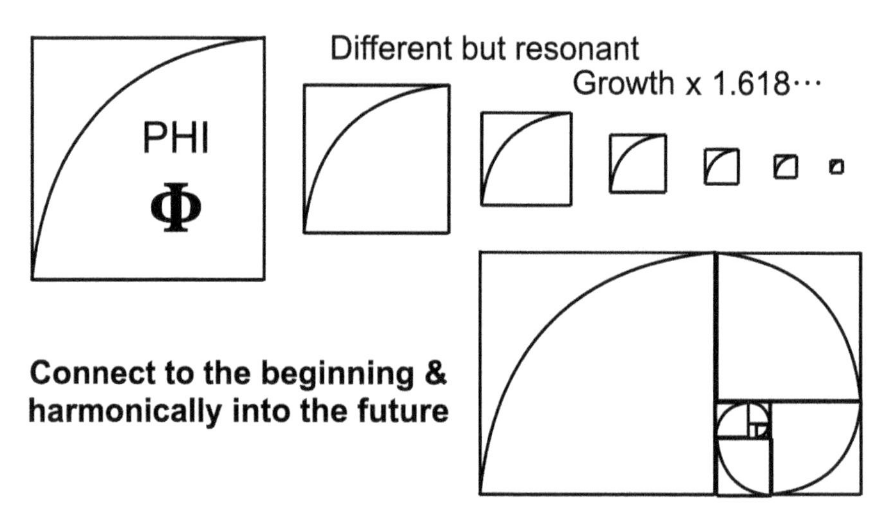

Fig. 6-4

Growth is change, but with the phi ratio we see how relationship is the cornerstone. (Fig. 6-4) The order of growth following **Φ** has every segment different, but harmonically resonant with the piece that came before, all the way back to the origination. It's connected to the past and fully present with its next step predetermined infinitely into the future. To embody this relationship and this archetypal energy is to know fully who you are and where you come from as you step knowingly into your self-determined destiny.

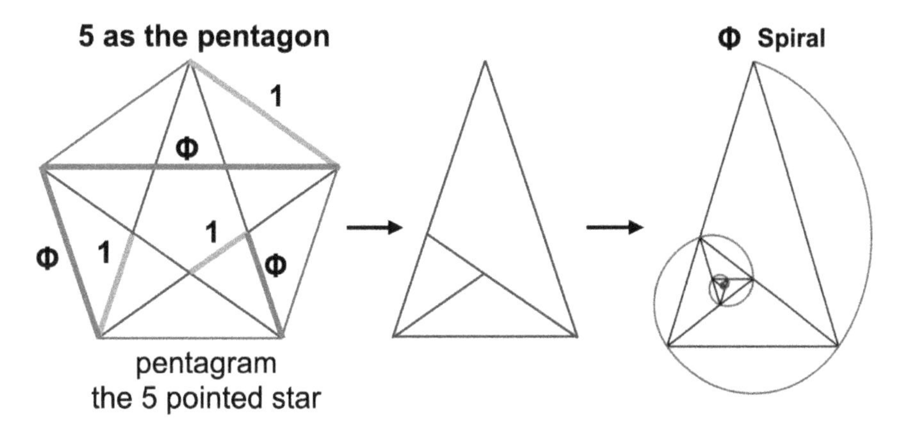

Fig. 6-5

The √5 and 5 as one of the Fibonacci numbers is certainly a nod to the importance of 5, but there is much more. If we create the 5-sided polygon called a pentagon and connect all of the corners, a 5-pointed star known as a pentagram is formed. We've now left the irrational aspect of phi behind and moved into a concrete expression of phi (**Φ**). As you can see in Fig. 6-5 the pentagram is full of phi ratio relationships as all the pieces of the pentagram can be broken apart and recombined to form phi ratio constructions. These pieces of the 5-pointed star aren't calculated individually or mathematically; they simply arise perfectly and accurately from the drawing itself. By drawing the curve, the phi ratio spiral once again works with the two triangles found at the center of the pentagon and the pentagram. A few times in the past I've come across a fearful reaction connected to the pentagram, 5-pointed star, because of its association with witchcraft. Sadly, this is a misplaced concern that stems from a lack of understanding. In the past, wise women used the life relational aspects of the phi ratio found within the pentagram to work with the natural order of life and healing since the proper tools designed using these principles can facilitate healing properties. The pentagram with a point downward meant the focus was earthward versus a celestial focus. Do you choose higher perspectives or are you content with focusing earthward?

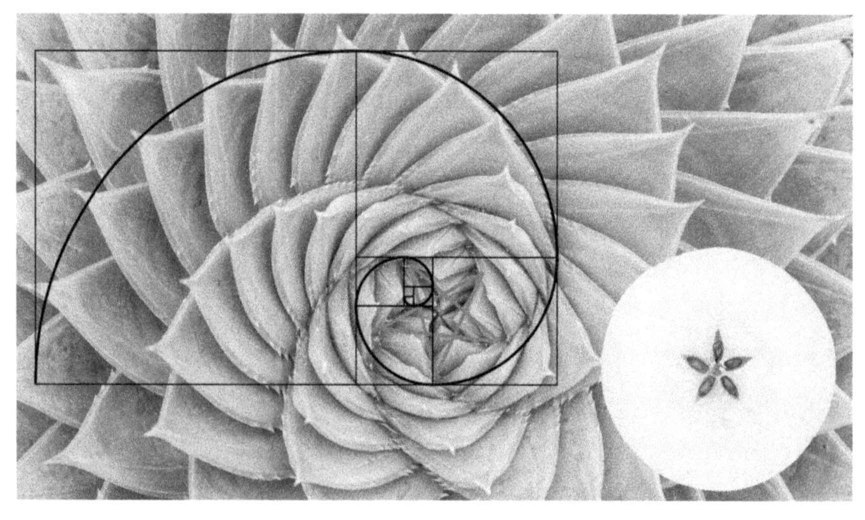

Fig. 6-6

With so many books and articles about the phi ratio, it sometimes appears to be the only mathematical concept governing growth, which is certainly not true. For example, the $\sqrt{3}$ is another irrational number that governs the display of 3- and 6-petaled flowers; however, the classic and most pervasive pattern of growth is found within the boundaries of phi. We need to understand it as an archetype, an ideal pattern behind creation that is utilized by environments and circumstance to allow for all the varieties we see between plants and animals of the same species.

Embedded in the phi pattern of how life grows is consciousness. It is our consciousness that can recognize beauty. It is natural and desirable to recognize beauty, whether it's a rose we admire or its delicious fragrance. It does something for us. It allows us to connect and helps us appreciate a purity that speaks to our hearts that can change the way we feel in a moment. That's why we think of beautiful flowers for giving a gift to somebody that we love because it magnifies universal beauty to touch each other with what Universe offers us.

> **Change and growth are the constant cycle of life, even if it causes discomfort. The phi ratio growth cycle lends understanding of where we came from and where we're going.**

The golden ratio is a precursor or seed of fractalization and holography. As a recent discovery, fractals show that the smallest part is still related to the biggest part. If you keep zooming in smaller and smaller, you continually come across the reoccurring pattern of the larger part that you began with. That's being demonstrated by these images of the Romanesco broccoli and a 5-pointed star in Fig. 6-7 that can add the same pattern larger or smaller indefinitely. Notice how the broccoli and the succulent in Fig. 6-6 grow in a spiral fashion. Number 5 works perfectly with the understanding of "as above, so below." This demonstrates the various vibrational patterns of creation that remain the same on a macro or micro scale, aligning with the same energy harmonic.

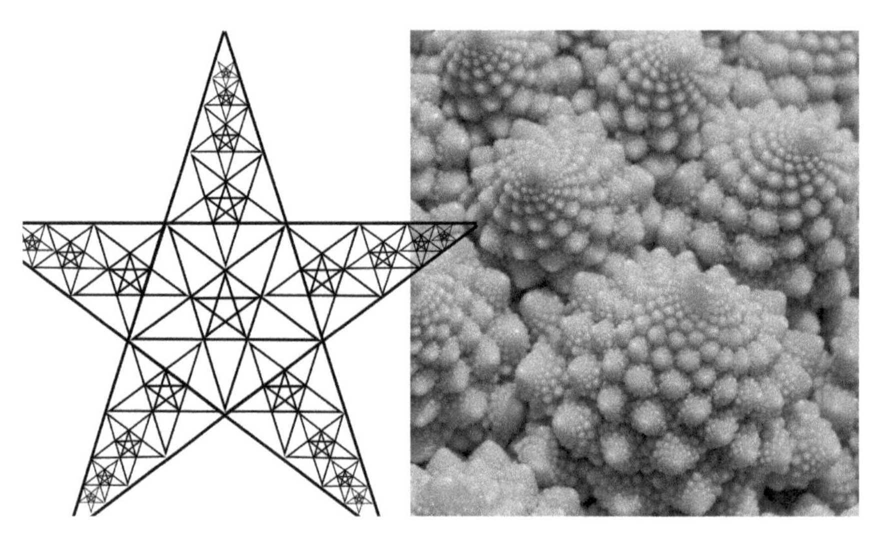

Fig. 6-7

The discovery of holograms offered new ways to conceptualize our reality. When a hologram has a small piece of it cut off, that small piece still contains all the elements of the total piece. It may not have as much clarity, but it's all there. Seven hundred years before we created the first hologram, a true sense of our holographic nature was eloquently expressed by the 13th-century poet Rumi:

> ***You are not a drop in the ocean; you are the ocean in a drop.***

This is what our geometric understanding of the sacred is leading us to: Your opportunity to be the ocean in a drop

Expanding consciousness is moving into a position where you allow the entire ocean to come into your awareness and source your ability to co-create. To create a Universal archetype in your environment is to invite the ocean in.

THE GREAT YEAR

In 2012, quite a stir went through the new age community when it was announced that the Mayan calendar was ending. It turned out to be more of a reset, like our new year celebration saying goodbye to the old year. What made the Mayan reset more unusual was the fact that it was dealing with a period of time equal to about 26,000 years. This large number of years causes most people to pause. How could they track such large periods of time and why?

In 1977, *Hamlet's Mill*, written by Giorgio De Santillana and Hertha Von Dechend, was published.[8] It was a very scholarly book dealing with the transfer of vital knowledge through myths shared worldwide over recorded history. The time and place of the myth could vary by thousands of years and be on opposite sides of the planet, but what tied them together was the use of the same numbers and measures. In deciphering the meanings, the authors concluded that the knowledge carried forward was aligned with an advanced understanding and focus on the 25,920-year precession of the equinoxes.

---

8 Giorgio De Santillana and Hertha Von Dechend, *Hamlet's Mill* (Boston: David R. Godine, 1977).

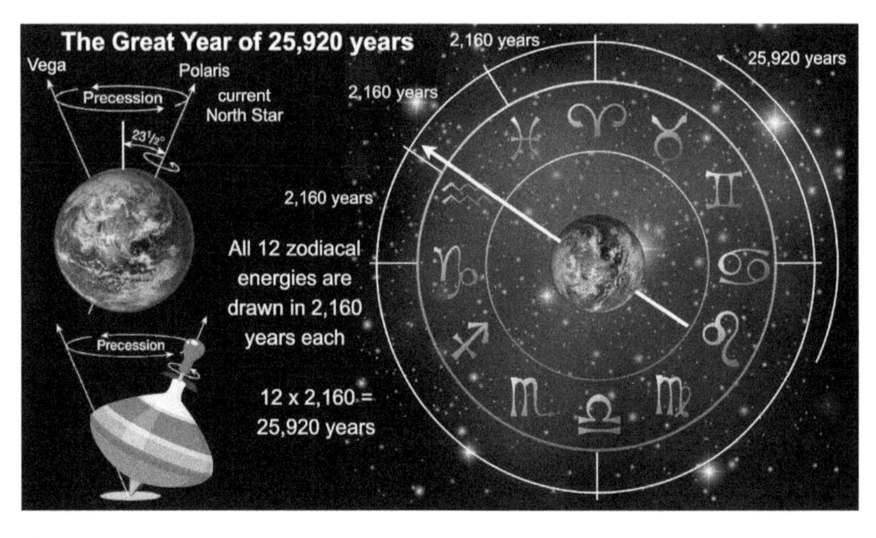

Fig. 6-8

This is a real mouthful of words and totally meaningless to most modern readers. In the preceding chapter, we talked about our year being broken into quarters based on the sun's shortest and longest appearances of daylight, which are known as the solstice and the equinox twice a year when day and night are equal. To most ancient cultures, these were important times to observe, being fixed times from year to year. Monuments such as Stonehenge in England were built to align with the sun's rising position on these important time markers. If the sacred site was built well, the sun always showed up in the exact same spot, unwavering from one year to the next, but something else changed. Looking up into the sky at the end of that day, far past where the sun would be, the background of stars was not the same as the year before. The movement was slight, very slight, because it took 72 years of earth time to shift the relationship of the stars in the background just one degree. Since there are

360° in a complete circuit, 72 years x 360° = 25,920 years for the north pole of Earth, which is used as a pointer to circle through all the signs of the zodiac.

The north pole changes its orientation over time because it wobbles just like a toy top that makes little circles with its top stem as it slows down. Currently, Polaris is the star that the north pole points toward. In 12,000 years, the slight wobble of the earth will create a new north star for us by the name of Vega. It's been our north star before, but that was about 14,000 years ago. This movement of our starry sky relative to fixed points on the Earth became known as the precession of the equinoxes, those times of the year that initiate spring and fall.

As the Earth spins on its axis, a vortex is created that passes through the north pole pulling energy into our planet that affects vibrational harmonics globally. (Fig. 6-8) Thus, the direction of our north pole passing through each of the 12 zodiac signs has a strong effect on all earth life for a period of about 2,160 years, which is referred to as an *age*. According to many scholars, we are in the process of leaving the Age of Pisces, where the symbol was a pair of fish, and its beginning was roughly aligned with the birth of Jesus Christ. In the late 1960s, the musical *Hair* hit Broadway with a song describing our transition into the dawning of the Age of Aquarius. This is part of a major flux point that we find ourselves moving through according to many belief systems.

Is the Great Year resetting now?

- Mayan Fifth World began in 2012.
- Hopi, Navaho, and Tibetan prophesies speak of the Fifth World Hoop soon beginning.

- Egyptians quartered their Great Year and link it to the rebirth of man as Aquarius in spring.
- Carried by the Romans, modern astrologers recognize the move into the age of Aquarius.
- Scholars of ancient Sanskrit say we are in the twilight of the Kali Yuga, the age of density.

Many of the myths described in *Hamlet's Mill* unmistakably refer to the passage of time through the Great Year of 25,920 years. The question is: Who could have figured this out so accurately? One degree star movement in 72 years would be almost impossible to detect without sophisticated equipment and a scientific understanding of earth rotational dynamics that rivals our own. It was with this logic that Graham Hancock drew upon the information found in *Hamlet's Mill* as pointing toward an advanced civilization that flourished alongside less advanced hunter gathers for thousands of years before their final destruction in 9,600 BC. This is only one of many pieces of information that he draws upon to support his conclusion, but to us viewing reality through the lens of Sacred Geometry, this special list of numbers offers some additional insights. It's exciting to examine them with fresh eyes that may offer a deeper vision into the thoughts and technologies of an ancient and advanced civilization whose seeds of awareness were passed down through generations.

Here is the list of numbers that they distilled:

- 360° = one yearly cycle – (36)
- 25,920 years (grand year)/360° = 72 years for each degree – (72)

- Great year divided into 12 parts of 30° each = 2,160 years – (12) & (216)

Two additional numbers that were commonly seen were 108 and 432. These were added to the list, believing 108 to be the sum of 36 and 72, and the number 432 was recognized as two parts of the 12-segmented Great Year (216 + 216 = 432).

This offered the final list: 12 – 36 – 72 – 108 – 216 – 432

> ***Anytime these numbers were used it was assumed by the authors and other researchers, that the Great Year and the precession of the equinoxes was being referenced.***

Now we're going to step into our geometer's perspective and revisit these important numbers starting with numeric progressions. We want to call in the genius of Nickola Tesla, who said 3, 6, and 9 were crucial for universal understanding. In Chapters 4 and 5, it became evident that the number 3 generated all sacred numbers.

$3^2 = 9$ is the first seed, and $3^3 = 27$ is the second seed to be continually doubled in order to maintain harmonic resonance.

- $3^2 = 9$ (× 2 progression) = 18 – 36 – 72 – 144 – 288
- $3^3 = 27$ (× 2 progression) = 54 – 108 – 216 – 432
- $3^3 = 27$ (× 2 progression) = 54 (18+36) – 108 (36+72) – 216 (72 + 144) – 432 (144 + 288)

Full 9 progression

- 18 – 36 – 54 – 72 – 108 – 144 – 216 – 288 – 432

Hamlet's Mill

- 12 – 36 – 72 – 108 – (total 36 + 72) – 216 – 432

When the products of the 3^2 progression are added together in pairs, such as 18 + 36 = 54, we get all the numbers in the 3^3 progression. This creates the full 9 progression of all the sacred numbers. This full list covers the numbers of *Hamlet's Mill* and adds several important ones as we will discover.

SPACE AND TIME HARMONICALLY RESONATE WITH EACH OTHER

From our geometer's perspective, space and time are more than intertwined, as Einstein suggested; they harmonically resonate with each other. As we shared in the last chapter the vibrational fields of different geometries measured in degrees have reflective numerical harmonics in time as measured in minutes, hours, and years. All the numbers of the 9 progression reveal themselves in chronological order as we list the polygons and platonic solids in ascending order of complexity and number of degrees. Not only do the geometries match up with the 9 progression, but the whole number multipliers used to equal the great year add more of these same numbers.

Precession of the Equinoxes = 25,920 years (Great Year)

Polygons and Solids	Degrees	Equals great year	9 progression	Hamlet's Mill
triangle	180°	X 144	18	12
square	360°	X 72	36	36
pentagon	540°	X 48	54	
hexagon	720°	X 36	72	72
octagon	1080°	X 24	108	108
tetrahedron	720°	X 36	144	
hexahedron	2160°	X 12	216	216
octahedron	1440°	X 18	288	
icosahedron	3600°	X 7.2	432	432
dodecahedron	6480°	X 4		

The Universe is operating on precise relationships that repeat themselves again and again. Of course, every geometry and division of the Great Year reduces to 9, as 9 is the container of all sacred numbers, and all sacred numbers rest evenly in the cradle of time. It is interesting to note that in some cases where decimals are used, a relevant sacred number still reveals itself as seen with the multiplier of the icosahedron being 7.2 compared to the often seen 72.

Time has a powerful relationship to physical space as defined by geometry. We see a consistent pattern of numbers that are defining both space and time. This offers us an understanding of where we are, where we have been and where we are going. The cosmic alignments interpreted through astrology have very particular angles, speeds, and alignments that affect our personalities and life path. As noted in the chart above, the total degrees of the dodecahedron evenly quarters the Great Year, creating four seasons similar to what happens during a year on earth. Randall Carlson has catalogued major earth shifts and found they are grouped around these quarterly transition times. Again, we see time linked to a geometry giving substance and verification to the relationship of a geometric view of our space/time continuum.

What is it about this part of the sequence (36 – 54 – 72 – 108) that has compelled civilizations and religions to keep them alive in our awareness for the last 11,000 years?

- 108 prayer beads are on the Malas of the Tibetan and Chinese Buddhists, the Taoists, Hindus, and Sikhs.
- Roman Catholics use a rosary of exactly half that, equaling 54 beads.
- We find 54 letters in the Sanskrit alphabet and 54 intersections in the Shri Yantra.
- Many ancient Roman temples had 108 columns supporting their roofs and Islam recognizes that 108 refers to God.
- Especially in Hinduism one sees it everywhere: 108 gopis, 108 holy places, 108 Upanishads and it goes on and on, but no one really has a clear understanding of why.
- Osiris murdered by 72 assassins, in Kabbalah, there are 72 names of God, 72 languages spoken at Babel, 72 archons in Gnosticism, 72 disciples of Confucius
- The ancient ruins of Angkor Wat have 5 gates with the entering avenues bordered by 54 statues on each side for a total of 108 per road and 540 stone deities overall.

These secrets were hidden in plain sight, very precisely so they wouldn't be forgotten. The use of these numbers by the ancients was considered holy and became embedded into religious objects and temples where they were deemed sacred. The number of mala beads (108) were a way to remember. The number is not being used in any practical way other than a remembrance. Any meaning beyond being a sacred number has been lost.

Here is another use of these numbers by one of the oldest and most mysterious secret societies in China, known as the Hung League. It's a repository for very ancient spiritual understanding, as well as ancient numbers. What is the meaning of this ancient initiation ritual?

> Q. What did you see on your walk?
> A. I saw two pots with red bamboo.
> Q. Do you know how many plants there were?
> A. In one pot were 36 and in the other 72 plants, together 108.
> Q. Did you take home some of them for your use?
> A. Yes, I took home 108 plants.
> Q. How can you prove that?
> A. I can prove it by verse.
> Q. How does this verse run?
> A. The red bamboo from Canton is rare in the world.
> In the groves are 36 and 72.
> Who in the world knows the meaning of this? When we have set to work, we will know the secret.

The last line makes it clear that this information will reveal itself when we use it or "set to work" with it. This can only occur when it enters the physical dimension by adding degrees to all the numbers. In Fig. 6-9 we have something that we can relate to, a 5-sided pentagon that embodies all these numbers in its internal angles. Furthermore, in the Hung ritual we see the description of the only two triangles in existence that create the phi ratio (36° – 72° – 72°) and (36° – 36° – 108°) where the short side is given the value of one and divided into the long side to reveal the phi ratio of 1.6180339···. The ratio that supports life and the evolution of consciousness. On the far right you can see how these two phi triangles embed one within the other alternating positions as they shrink or expand infinitely.

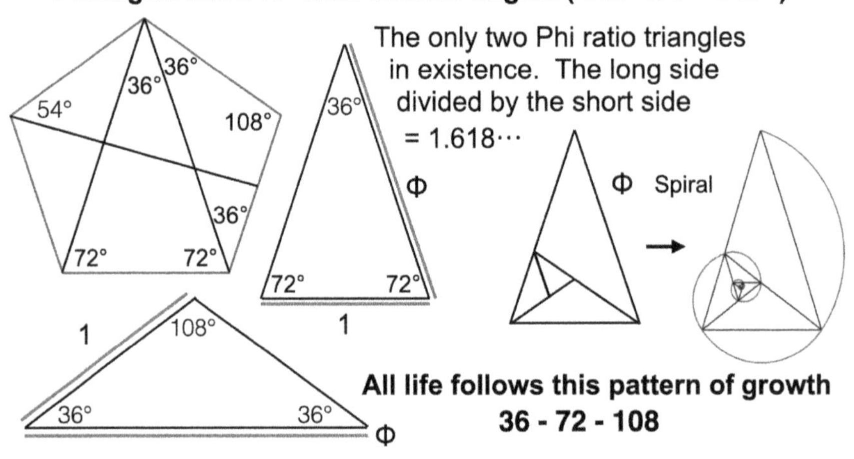

Fig. 6 - 9

We can take the pentagon, which is the generator of these phi ratios, multiply it by 12 and fold it up into the fifth platonic solid, the dodecahedron. In 2003 scientists revealed that Universe is finite and shaped like a dodecahedron. Fig. 6-10 (New findings in 2003 based on the study of data from NASA's Wilkinson Microwave Anisotropy Probe [WMAP] on cosmic background radiation reveal that Universe is finite and shaped like a dodecahedron.) We live within a Universe focused on the phi ratio and its use in the creation of life.

Mathematicians looking at planetary orbits around the sun have discovered that if Mercury is given a value of one, then the average proportional increment value of all the planets out to Pluto averages to phi, 1.6180339···. If Earth's orbit is given a value of one, then five of the closest planets have orbits proportional to multiples of phi. They are vibrating with the field of energy, incubating life, and as planetary bodies in our solar system, they are helping to step down this energy to make it more available to life on Earth. They help to focus and ground archetypal energies.

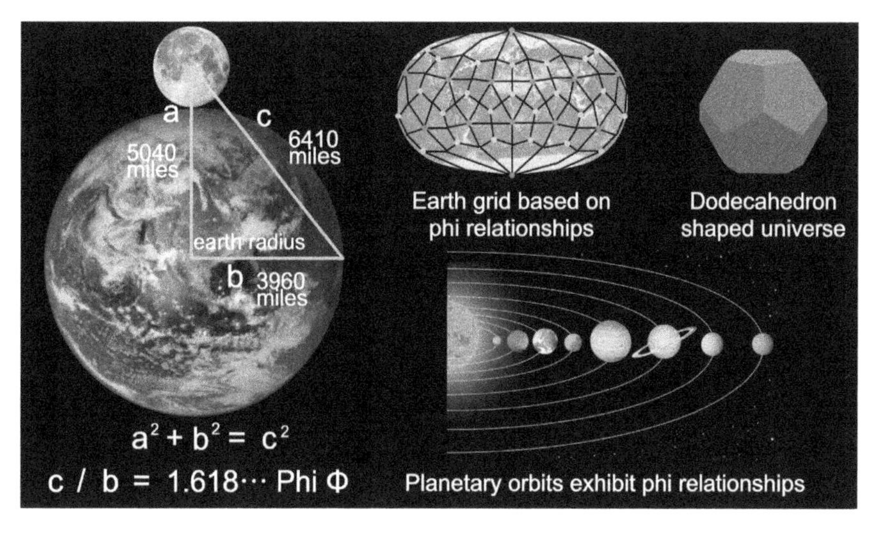

Fig. 6-10

One of the strongest fields of support comes from our planet's dance with the moon. As seen in Fig. 6-10 we place the moon so it is adjacent to the Earth and create a large right- angle triangle connecting the centers of the moon and Earth with the Earth's edge and back to the moon center. We can use the Pythagorean theorem (a2 + b2 = c2) for right-angle triangles and fill in the known radius measures for the Earth and moon to discover the length of the hypotenuse or slanted edge from the moon to Earth's equator. When we divide that line (c) by the radius of the Earth, we get 1.6180339···, the phi ratio. The Earth and moon are interacting together to vibrate with the life evolving phi ratio.

In the 1980s, Russian scientists mapped the energetic grid of the planet and found it to be best represented by the interlocking relationship of a dodecahedron and an icosahedron, which creates phi ratio relationships in the way energy flows through the planetary grid or earth circulatory system.

Is it any wonder that the ancients wanted to bring attention and focus to the value of phi ratio constructions? If we want to be aligned with the rhythm of Universe and be supported by the pulse of life for our health and mental well-being then it is imperative that we find ways to bring these universal energies into our environment.

TAKE A MOMENT TO REFLECT . . .

We are here in a Universe of precise structure and order that operates this physical reality. Everything begins with pure formless energy, and for creation to function it follows angles and patterns that result in exquisite designs on this earth. The vast variety of lifeforms are all related in the way they are structured. It is an amazing display of unity. Nature shows us an abundance of beauty and harmony.

When we look deeply, we recognize how our consciousness interacts with everything around us. We create a crucial focus that is part of evolution. As we expand our awareness, we can use this knowledge in creating our lives to become divine partners with Spirit. We can impress life with compassion and loving consciousness for positive outcomes rather than chaos. What we experience as chaos and dysfunction is a result of being disconnected and out of balance.

Consciousness is energetically connected to all that is and an essential part of how this Universe evolves. We are co-creators, not just receivers of what we see around us. Feel at home here on Earth as you breathe in the creative resonance of love. Feel its enlivening and nurturing energy. Fill yourself with gratitude for your life, loved ones and the possibilities you are creating for a more compassionate, prosperous, and loving path.

Feel your heart opening as you rhythmically breathe and become more centered. Let your mind drift and be directed by your soul. Enjoy the love and wisdom within you. This state brings you greater peace, abundance, and happiness for the good of all. Trust your intuition, inner voice, and inner vision. Relax into the presence of your true nature within your body now, embracing the deep connection you have to Universe and all souls on this planet.

CHAPTER 7
6 BRINGS STRUCTURE, FUNCTION, AND ORDER TO SPACE/TIME

The number 6 brings structure, function, and order to the inseparable space-time continuum. From molecules to planets, 6 is the way nature frequently chooses to build. Physical matter relies on 6 for its structure using the six-sided hexagon for strength as well as making sure all the parts fit together.

Remember when we were explaining the triangle, and the strength that 3 created? Of all the polygons, it's the strongest. Number 6 depends upon the triangle for strength in two ways. Cut the hexagon point to point like a pie into six triangular sections or connect every other point, to get a 6-pointed star made from two triangles with one pointing up and the other pointing downward. In both cases we see the strength of 6 as a hexagon comes from multiple triangles formed within.

By following the patterns displayed throughout creation, we're given a set of design instructions on how best to build and live optimally. It's part of the master plan that's been hidden in plain sight.

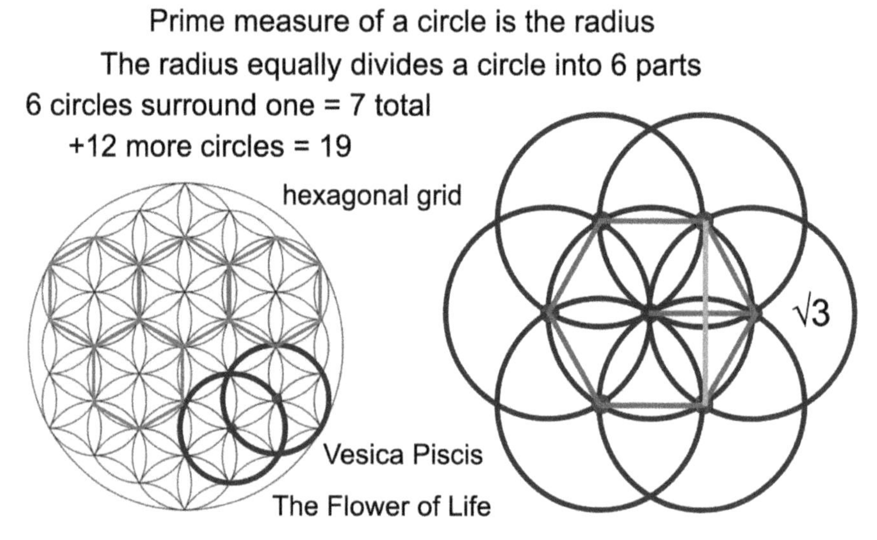

Fig. 7-1

The number 6 doesn't just bring physical order; it *is* the order within all space and time. It is birthed directly by the circle of Source, Fig. 7-1, whose only measure is its radius. As children, many of us have played with a compass to draw a circle and then using that same measure, placed the point of the compass on the edge of the circle to mark off 6 even divisions. If we connect the segments, we form a hexagon with all the edges equal to the radius of the circle that created it. If we choose to draw circles at each segment mark, it's almost miraculous to see a perfect six-petalled flower grow with just a compass as the tool. Many of us didn't want to stop and placed the compass point where the circles crossed for two more sequences of 6 circles each. This creates a two-dimensional form called the Flower of Life, made from 19 overlapping circles. It's one of the first geometries made using only a compass and owes its notoriety to two things. First, dozens of vesica piscis lie within the outer circle, and each one is responsible for generating all the square roots needed for creation. Second, it forms a hexagonal grid, and most natural patterns and geometries fit into a hex grid.

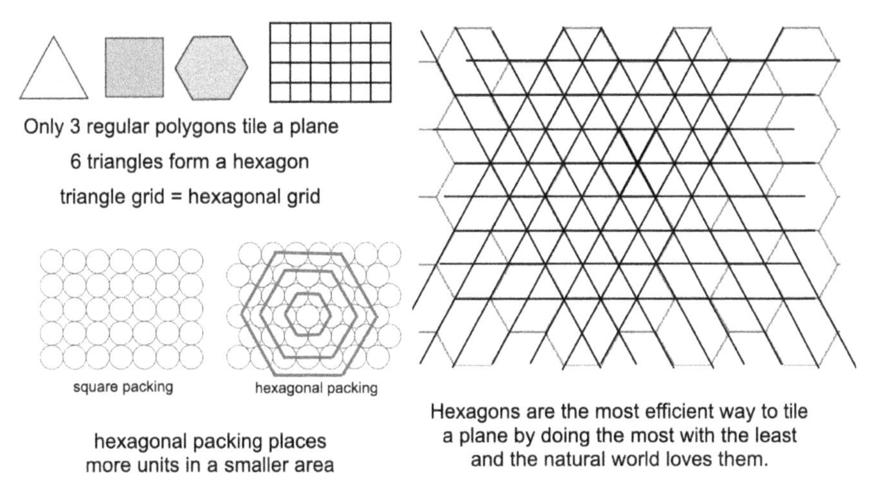

Fig. 7-2

Let's explore more about grids that fill a plane in Fig. 7-2. If you take a sheet of paper and you want to evenly cover it with polygons so there are no gaps, there are only 3 regular polygons that can do it, the triangle, square, and hexagon. To cover a plane so all the shapes fit tightly together is called tessellation. Squares are the easiest for us to use in building as seen in most bathrooms, showers, and kitchens. We mostly use squares in what we build, but in the natural world, that's a different story.

If you use 6 triangles to tile a plane they form a hexagon, so in essence triangles grow into hexagons, which leaves us with only squares or hexagons to tile a plane. Hexagons contain the triangles and become the most efficient way for Universe to fill space. If you look closely at the square packing of circles in Fig. 7-2 you see that packing any shape that is not a square, leaves a lot of gaps and wasted space. The packing example on the right shows hexagonal packing, which is the most efficient way to pack. You can get more items in the same amount of space. Universe loves this economy, so it uses hexagons everywhere.

You can do the most with the least, and the natural world uses these principles in the way it creates from the face of a pineapple, where all the segments are hexagons to the compound eyes of insects, as seen in Fig. 7-3 and Fig. 7-4. When you look closely at the hexagons created by 6-petaled flowers you'll notice that the petals are never evenly dispersed. They're always one set of 3 petals above another set of 3 petals. In the case of the iris on the right, the 3 that are on top are quite different from the 3 that are on the bottom. Here nature is showing us that 6 is composed of 3 plus 3 and also that she likes to progress in petal quantities following the Fibonacci series: 1,1,2,3,5,8,13,21···

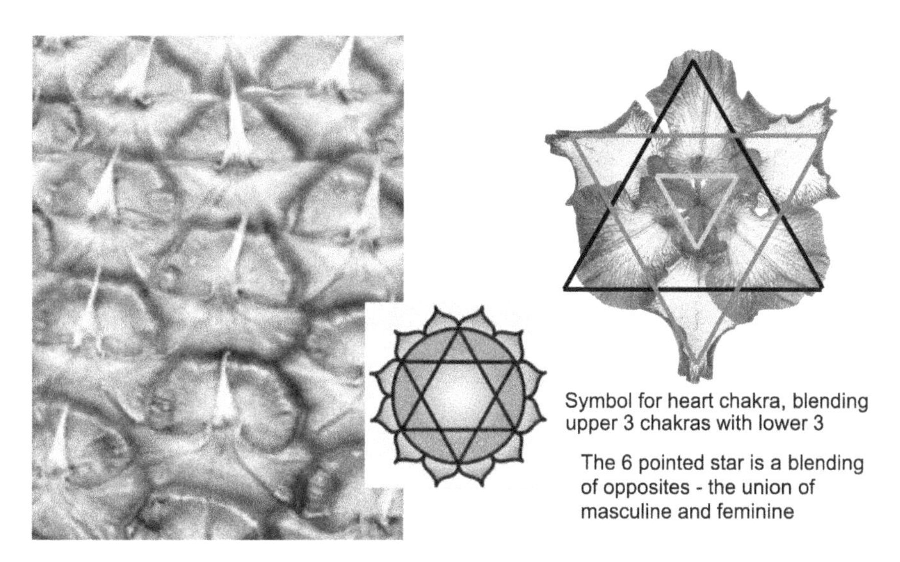

Fig. 7-3

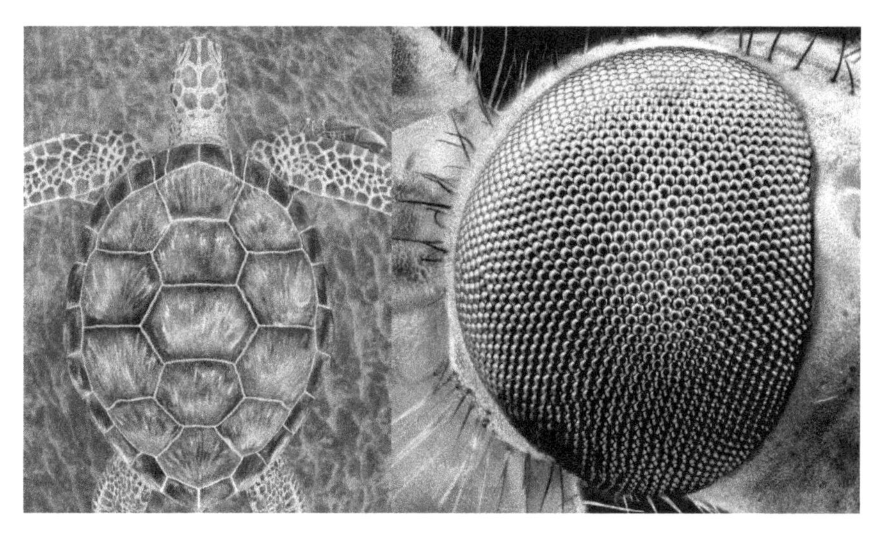

Fig. 7-4

Eastern philosophies have symbolic images for each of the 7 chakras, and the center heart chakra is represented by a 6-pointed star. The star blends the upper 3 chakras—crown, third eye, and throat with the bottom 3 chakras—root, sacral, and solar plexus. Everything is balanced in the heart. They understood that the 6-pointed star is about balance and the blending of higher and lower: as above, so below. It brings opposites together, such as the downward-pointing feminine triangle with the upward-pointing masculine triangle. Their union has come to be known as the Latin word for 6, which happens to be *sex*.

Sometimes it's more than just a universal shape that is reflected in creation, as is the case with the hexagonal plates found on the shells of turtles. A number of ancient cultures from Norsemen to American Indians used a turtle shell as their yearly calendar. The 13 large plates in the middle of the shell represented the year's 13 moon cycles and the 28 small segments found around the outside rim reflected the number of days in each moon cycle for a total of 364 days plus one day of rest giving us our modern calendar equivalent. The physical design reflects the natural order of time. By adopting a 12-month year, we've abandoned natural patterns to form an artificial construct that separates us from Universal pattern. Not a big step, as some would argue, but one step following another has led us from the natural and connected rhythms of the sun, moon, and stars into a world of our own creation reflecting disconnection and separation.

THE ROLE OF CARBON

Everything alive is built from atoms of carbon. The study of carbon's role in life is called organic chemistry as opposed to everything else being inorganic chemistry. Carbon's dominant presence is due to the number of different bonds it can make (4) with other elements, forming long chains of atoms offering over a million different carbon compounds. Every compound connected to life begins with a hexagonal ring of 6 carbon atoms called a benzine ring, Fig. 7-5. Groupings of these rings are often referred to by chemists as turtle shells, with the micro world of atoms reflecting the macro world we can touch.

On the lefthand side of Fig. 7-5 is a chalkboard full of different molecules where the hexagonal carbon rings are paired with hydrogen, oxygen, and nitrogen to form organic molecules called hydrocarbons. The same elements are used again and again to create the four basic types of molecules used for all of life. It is the variation of their combined shapes that determine their function. Pattern defines reality and function follows form.

Of the four types used by lifeforms, one grouping pattern creates proteins that do the work of a cell. Another forms nucleic acid, which is the "N" in DNA and is responsible for carrying all the information. Cholesterol, hormones, and all the fats are made of carbon chains called lipids and the final massive set of carbon molecules needed for life are called carbohydrates; they provide all the energy for a body and store it in the form of sugars.

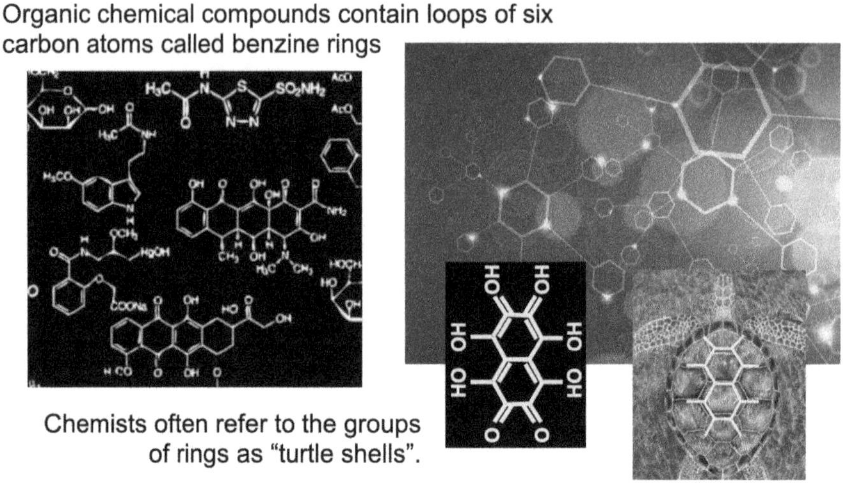

Organic chemical compounds contain loops of six carbon atoms called benzine rings

Chemists often refer to the groups of rings as "turtle shells".

Fig. 7-5

A rare and different form of carbon molecule that was recently discovered in 1985 is seen in Fig. 7-6. It was predicted by Bucky Fuller and resembles some of his geodesic domes, so it was named in his honor. The C-60 buckminsterfullerene is made from 60 carbon atoms folded into a ball made of 20 hexagons and 12 pentagons like a soccer ball, which brings together the energy of the 5 and the 6. Several of the images in Fig. 7-6 are different perspectives of the C-60 molecule that we make in gold-plated bronze, because it is one of the highest vibrational forms of carbon interlinked with all life. On the physical level it is used as one of the most powerful and smallest antioxidants known for being the only one capable of traveling through cell walls and the brain/blood barrier.

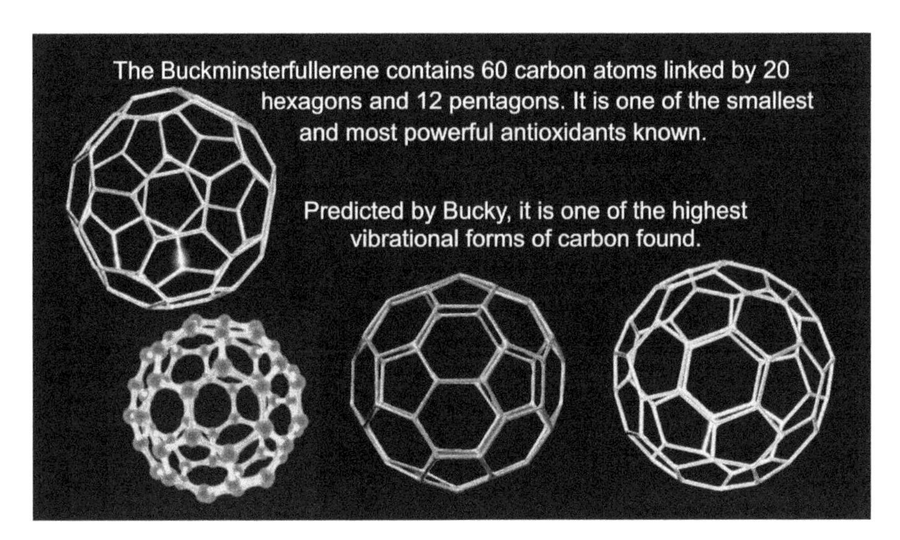

Fig. 7-6

> *Geometry reveals the underlying harmony and order that exist in the universe. It is a tool for uncovering the mysteries of creation.*
>
> *– R. Buckminster Fuller*

Number 6 is everywhere. You can't build a Universe without it.

Here are some amazing facts we've been covering:
The 2D 6-sided hexagon = 720° (6 angles of 120° each) The 3D tetrahedron = 720°
The sun, moon, Earth, and geometric solids are all evenly divisible by the base harmonic of 720.

The angles of the phi ratio triangles are multiples of 6 and 6^2. From organic life to the inorganic crystal kingdom, 6 is the universal principle for structure and order.

On the left side of Fig. 7-7 you have hexagons of carbon forming layers or sheets of graphite that can easily slide off the tip of a pencil to leave its mark on a sheet of paper. On the right of this illustration, the same carbon atoms rearrange their molecular structure as fractal stacks of tetrahedrons, each with six edges, forming one of the hardest substances, a diamond. The underlying reason for the strength of the diamond is because its tetrahedral molecules create the strongest geometry. The large tetrahedron is made up of smaller and smaller tetrahedrons that build this nearly indestructible form. As the groups of 6 change their form, the function of the molecule changes too because of the underlying shape.

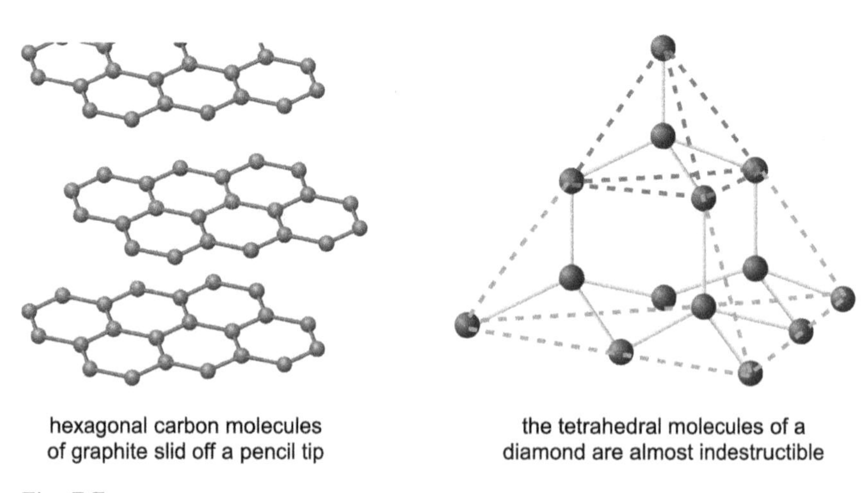

Fig. 7-7

In fig. 7-8 we see how 6 displays itself in the natural world. As bees build honeycombs, they're forced by that higher knowing we call instinct to use the most efficient way of building cells next to each other, which is hexagonal packing. In this image, two different types of crystalline structures create hexagonal geometries. The clear crystals of silicon dioxide are formed from tetrahedral groupings of molecules twisting up long 6-sided columns as they grow with trillions of molecules replicating the same structure that is reflected in the 6-sided crystal we see in our macroworld. Crystals often produce an energetic sensation when they are directed toward the body partially because their long spiraling shafts are replicated trillions and trillions of times magnifying the effect. These duplications create a stronger resonant field similar to a radio telescope array where many individual antennas are able to focus as one large unit.

The dark basalt columns at the bottom of Fig. 7-8 are formed as lava cools under the right conditions to allow 6-sided columns to form. Cooling temperatures often force symmetry into the environment as matter searches for efficient and ordered ways to regroup. Snowflakes form lacy 6-sided displays when temperatures drop below freezing.

Fig. 7-8

CONSCIOUSNESS INSTRUCTS WHAT MANIFESTS ON PLANET EARTH

As mentioned in Chapter 5, the Japanese scientist Dr. Masaru Emoto demonstrated through his work with water how positive intent could be held by water to transform its purity. Water vibrationally enhanced by focusing positive thoughts of love and joy created more beautiful and perfectly formed snowflakes than unenhanced water. He found that it was even possible to take polluted water that couldn't form more than an ice blob and enhance its vibrational nature through focused intent to form lovely snowflakes. In each of these cases, the perfection of the geometry as witnessed in the snowflake reflected the clarity of the thought. This is one of many confirmations that when we are in sync with the essence of creation, we can direct that level of consciousness into something, and powerful transformations can occur. Within our lives, when we operate from clear intent, we affect the outcome. We alter what's going on in the moment when we change the feelings that have been coloring a relationship with someone. That's why we believe this work is so important. It's showing us how Universe operates, giving us a toolbox to evolve and make changes, not only in our personal lives, as it also impacts the rhythms of this Universe. As Dr. Emoto demonstrated, when we project love, compassion, and joy into something, it transforms actual physical matter. We are living in a world that is more malleable and reflective of our consciousness than we may have believed.

When we project love and consciousness into something, we're not changing it per se, but allowing it to change. We're expanding the space to a field of higher possibility. When that field is raised in vibration, then the most beautiful expression of perfection can evolve. The individual work we do to raise our consciousness allows perfection to flourish in our bodies, relationships, and our environment.

CREATING GEOMETRIES

The geometries we create are based on the archetypal principles we've been discussing. An important part of the design process is for us to enter a higher level of consciousness through meditation and connecting to higher dimensions of soul. From this perspective, we touch on ways to develop tools for positively affecting people and our environment. We have found using a conductive material such as copper will easily resonate with archetypes of creation and holds the vibration that elevates how we feel and connect with the greater sphere of who we are. These three-dimensional tools (particularly when they are spinning) emanate a field that can clear and bring order to a space that may have been filled with chaos and discordant frequencies. Instead, it is building a field that offers infinite possibilities, allowing our consciousness to be expressed in a more expansive and loving way.

> ***Nature uses geometry as its organizing principle. From the structure of atoms to the shape of galaxies, everything follows geometric laws.***
>
> ***– R. Buckminster Fuller***

Creating geometries that are designed using patterns found in nature offers us a similar experience. When we are in a beautiful, peaceful place by a stream, it reduces the effects of stress, enhances creativity, and promotes a feeling of connection that positively affects our health and well-being. Hundreds of research studies are now providing evidence for what we have known intuitively for so long. Spending time in nature improves our mental and physical health both long and short term. One of the key reasons for the profound effect that nature has on us is that all the elements existing in a natural environment resonate with the higher universal archetypes of creation. It's what we are made of.

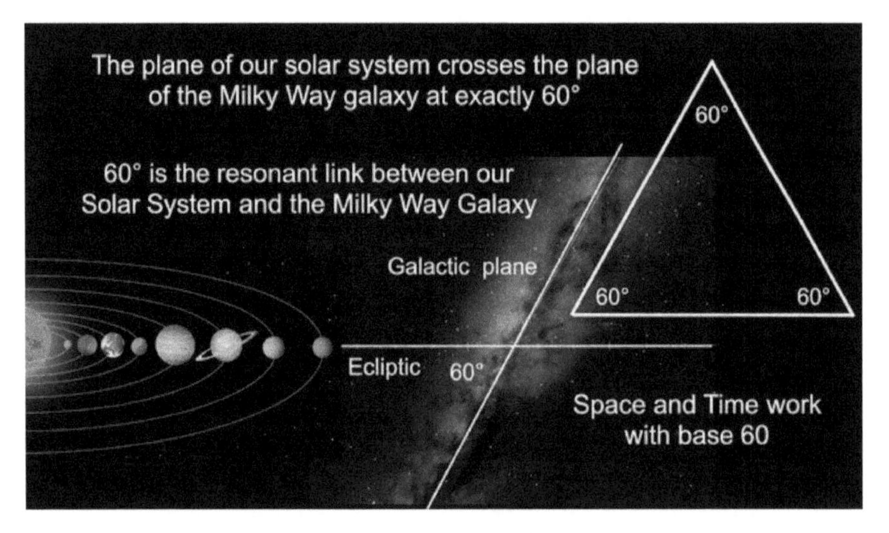

Fig. 7-9

Everything in our reality revolves around 60. Number 1 is divinity hidden, 10 is divinity expressed in the physical and 6 × 10 = 60 is the divine expression of 6. Our time, measure, and especially geometry are all resonant with 60.

The planets of our solar system orbit the sun in a flat plane like marbles on a plate, Fig. 7-9, which is referred to as an ecliptic.

The flat plane of our solar system crosses the plane of our Milky Way Galaxy at exactly 60° setting up the resonant frequency of our space-time continuum.

Science points back 5,000 years toward the Sumerians as using a base 60 counting system that carried forward to our present-day system of using 60 in tracking time and the measure of degrees in a circle. It's convenient to focus on them, but the truth is we are talking about divine archetypes as it regards our measure of time and degrees of space. The Sumerians didn't invent a successful measure, they discovered what already existed or, more than likely, it was passed down to them as the way Universe works.

I'm thankful that we are still using the same measures today. A base 10 system of dividing the circle would give us fractional degrees rather than whole numbers, but more importantly the base 60 system maintains harmonic resonance between our daily interactions and the cosmos.

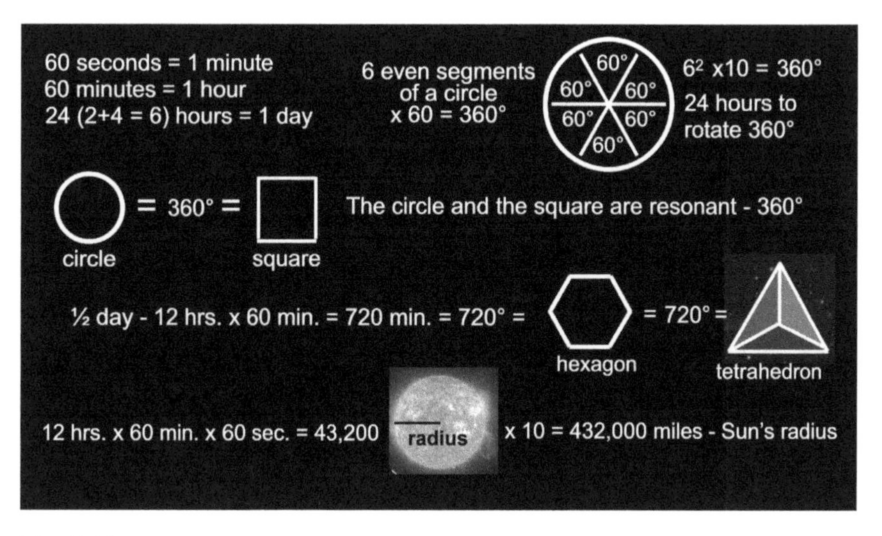

Fig. 7-10

Look at Fig. 7-10 to see how many times 60 and 6 are used with time. 60 x 6 gives us the number of degrees in a circle and square, creating resonance between heaven and earth.

The harmonics of time interweave with the degrees of space and the measure of the earth, moon, and sun in miles. Starting with half a day and then a full day, we will connect what the number of minutes or seconds in that period of time is harmonically resonant with. The symbol (↔) indicates numerical resonance between differing systems of measure, such as minutes to miles.

½ day – 12 hrs. × 60 min./hr. = 720 min. ↔ 720° = hexagon = tetrahedron
½ day – 43,200 sec. × 10 ↔ 432,000 miles = sun's radius 1 day – 1,440 min. ↔ 1440° = octahedron
1 day – 86,400 sec. × 10 ↔ 864,000 miles = sun's diameter

It is curious to note that half of our day cycle in seconds is equal to half the sun's diameter, while a full day of 86,400 seconds × 10 equals the sun's full diameter.

1½ days – 2,160 min. ↔ 2,160° = cube
↔ 2,160 miles = moon's diameter
↔ 2,160 years = astrological age
$6^3 = 2,160$

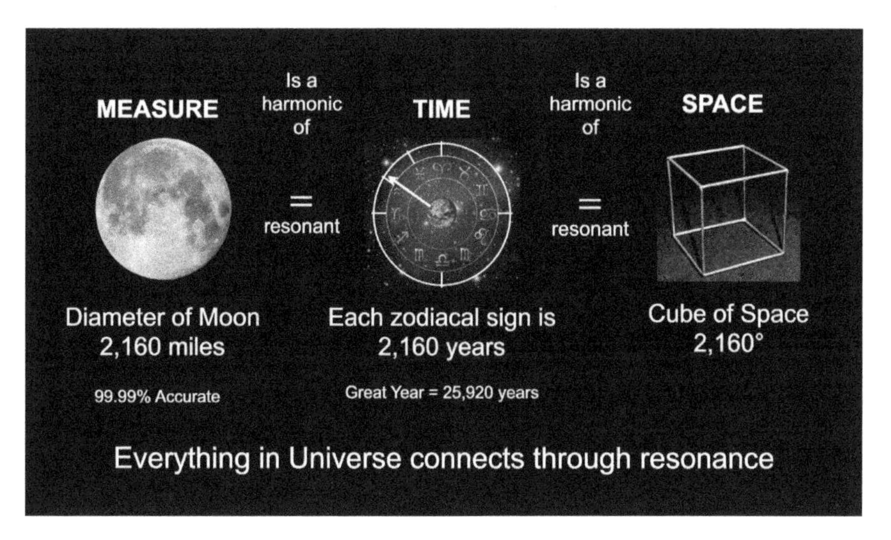

Fig. 7-11

As seen in Fig. 7-11 there is a harmonic relationship between the moon, astrological age, and a cube. The Universe depends upon harmonics to create relationships and coherence. When similar numbers occur over different measures, the resonant frequencies bring to light the underlying energetic web that has been built to direct the patterns of consciousness expressed. We may be an observer without analyzing the how or why. When enough relationships repeat themselves, we can learn from these parameters to build a similar natural resonance that overcomes the artificial constructs of modern technology that blocks the energetic flow of higher dimensional connection. Creating resonance in our environment will allow the energies associated with those harmonic frequencies to flow into our lives, overcoming stagnation and separation.

As we observe the effects of the same numbers being expressed as different measures it becomes apparent that a number is not a meaningless abstraction representing only a quantity. Rather, it is a universal frequency, a field of energy. This is the reason we have been discussing the characters and personalities of numbers. They have a life and rhythm that creates a vibrating field of attraction. When we witness seemingly different identifications like miles, years, and degrees that create harmonic relationships based on these specific numbers, we can recognize the hidden unity within the oneness of Universe. These are clues left for us so we might understand the resonant attractors we can choose to positively affect our ability to live harmoniously.

2½ days – 3,600 min. ↔ 3600° = icosahedron 1 hour – 3,600 sec. ↔ 3600° = icosahedron

3½ days – 5,040 min. ↔ 5,040 miles = Earth's radius + moon's radius

4½ days – 6,480 min. ↔ 6480° = dodecahedron
108 hours ↔ 108° = each of the 60 angles on a dodecahedron

5½ days – 7,920 min. ↔ 7,920 miles = Earth's diameter

6½ days – 9,360 min. ↔ 7,920 miles Earth's diam. + 1,440° octahedron

7½ days – 10,800 min. ↔ 10,800 miles = moon's diam. + sun's diam.

The sun's diameter is reduced two magnitudes (864,000 / 100 = 8,640) to be consistent with the moon 2,160 miles, which is 99.99 percent accurate.

All of these measurements are real; nothing is conjecture, fudged, or made up. However, the diameter of the Earth differs a bit from scientific measurements, so here is how we arrived at 7,920 miles for Earth's diameter.

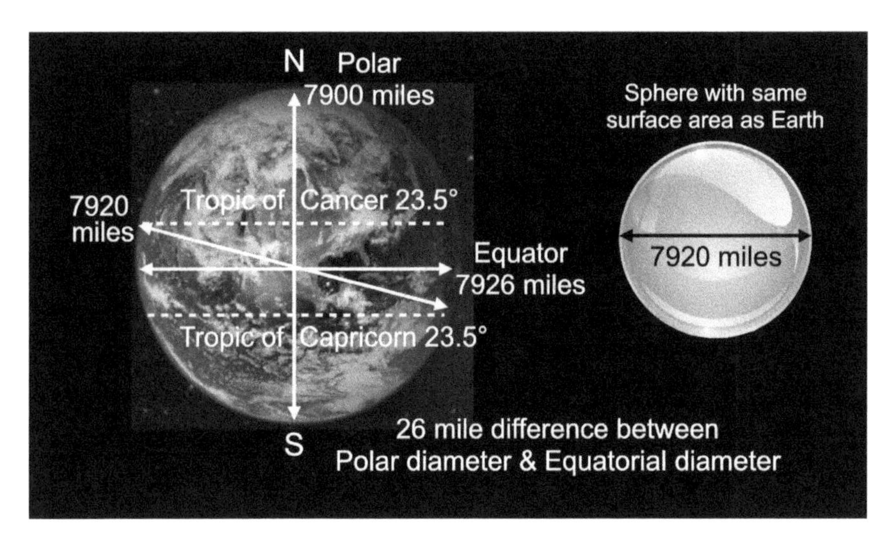

Fig. 7-12

In Fig. 7-12 the polar diameter is 7,900 miles, which is 26 miles less than our equatorial measurement of 7,926 miles. It is a very good thing that they aren't equal as Earth's thicker middle helps stabilize the planet as it spins like a toy top with a wider midsection. Above and below the equator at 23.5° North and 23.5° South are the Tropic of Cancer and the Tropic of Capricorn. If we draw a diagonal between the two latitudes compensating for the equatorial bulge by skipping above and below it, then we have a diameter of 7,920 miles. Archetypes are ideals; they represent perfection at the universal level. They are models for creation to aspire towards. If we were to take the Earth and mold it into a smooth ball with the same surface area, then the diameter of that perfect Earth would be 7,920 miles. (I first saw this explanation shared in a video by Randall Carlson.)

TAKE A MOMENT TO REFLECT . . .

Before there was a physical world, there was a flow of endless energy. There was nothingness, silence, stillness. Within that void is an eternal expression of consciousness, an extraordinary creative spirit that contains the urge to endlessly create a realm of life where all possibilities and blessings exist.

The number 6 carries the intent to build creation in an everlasting way with orderly patterns that exceed time and space. It is the perfect structural integrity for evolving a Universe that encompasses the multidimensions of life.

The vastness of creation is within you. Your mind, body, heart, and spirit are precisely designed to resonate with all life around you. The Universe is not only your home; it is you, and you are it. By following the patterns displayed throughout creation, we're given a set of instructions on how to build and live optimally. It's part of the master plan that's been hidden in plain sight.

The physical world is based on a structure born from consciousness. Our feelings, intents, thoughts, and actions give rise to the growth of this Universe. Each new form takes on a life that can evolve in a multitude of ways. Consciousness offers the resonance to inspire and direct creation, with love being the purest and highest influence.

As we embrace our role as divine co-creators, we can impress life with compassion and loving consciousness for the good of all. As we stay connected, we trust our relationship with Source and everything around us. Consciousness is the conductor that molds how this Universe evolves, and we are the rhythm that defines creation.

CHAPTER 8
UNIVERSAL HARMONICS AND ARCHETYPES

The first 6 numbers are the essential building blocks of creation.
Numbers 7, 8, and 9 create connections to the higher realms.

The number 7 personifies magic and the mysteries: 7 days of creation; 7 days of the week; 7 chakras; 7 musical notes; 7 colors of the rainbow; 7 sages. As shared by John Michell, "Everything that can be called sacred, and eternal is appropriately numbered in sevens."[9] One element is only the beginning. Number 7 speaks to incorporating the variations that contribute to the whole process. The 7 musical notes or colors of the rainbow allow us to appreciate the various aspects of light and sound that are essential elements of creation.

---

9 John Mitchell with Allan Brown, *How the World Is Made: The Story of Creation According to Sacred Geometry* (Rochester, VT: Inner Traditions, 2012), page 214.

Number 7 is also unique as a prime number that cannot be evenly divided by any number other than 1 and 7 itself. It begins the transition to higher realms and is seen as a numerical pivot point in sequences such as the one below:

$$1 \times 2 \times 3 \times 4 \times 5 \times 6 = 720 = 8 \times 9 \times 10$$
$$1 \times 2 \times 3 \times 4 \times 5 \times 6 \times 7 = 5{,}040 = 7 \times 8 \times 9 \times 10$$

We arrive at the important product of 720 by multiplying the first six numbers and the last three numbers of our base 10 system, but 7 must be left out of the mix. If we include 7 in both groups, we get a total of 5,040, which is the value of the radius of the moon plus the radius of the Earth.

The number 8 offers the playing field for creation and is often associated with concepts of balance, harmony, and infinity. When 8 is written horizontally it is formed by two connected loops, associated with the symbol for infinity and the concepts of boundlessness, continuity, and endless possibilities. The constructs of 8 powerfully bring together unrealized elements and opportunities for abundant ongoing life that can reach higher levels of potential through its maturation process. It is a bridge between the realms.

Sacred paintings and geometrically designed yantras from Tibetan Buddhism are often laid out on a background square with protruding "Ts" in the middle of each side forming a field of eight, as if a second square were turned 45° and laid over the first square with the points of the second square aligned with the "T"s where the energy is flowing. 8^2 offers the field upon which everything is played. It is the platform for reality to express itself:

64 squares on a chessboard; 64 possible arrangements of codons carrying information in DNA and the 64 hexagrams of the I-Ching, a system of divining higher knowledge. 64 reduces to 1, Unity, which further reinforces the metaphor for the singularity of the field/platform/system that supports the expression of this reality.

The arrangement of galaxies follows the edges of large octahedrons (the 8-sided platonic solid) as they are placed point to point forming structures like stacked egg cartons. These structures bring huge, heavenly bodies into a relatable structure, reflecting the importance of 8 as the universal playing field. However, as you will see in Fig. 8-1, octahedrons point to point are not a stable structure. They need the strength of a tetrahedron on each face whose points connect forming a cube. Three perspectives of this form referred to as Metatron's Cube can be seen in Fig. 8-2.

The number 9, the last number of our base 10 system, is often associated with completion and reaching the end of a cycle, including stages of growth, maturity, and wisdom. This highlights the evolutionary process to reach a pinnacle and go on to another step that may exist beyond what is known. Number 9 shows us there is an end in sight, yet it may only be an entrance to a higher order. This may be considered one of the most mystical numbers. Stacking the 9 numbers in groups of 3 forms a perfect

3 × 3 square in which 9 is the container of all the numbers. Laid out clockwise on a circle, the enneagram formed from the 9 numbers becomes a divining agent for understanding personality types. As we have already mentioned 9 is the container for the sacred, as all sacred numbers reduce to 9.

Geometry cannot be understood without recognizing the values of basic numbers that build a three-dimensional world. The numbers we've discussed carry significance in the physical world and beyond. Each of these numbers expand the container of conscious life with higher numbers inviting interaction with higher access. Our lives are multidimensional, which indicates there are realms beyond our physical senses. Senses like intuition, spiritual connection, and the sense of "knowing" are becoming more significant as we evolve into greater awareness. The first 3 numbers (1, 2, and 3) educate us about the origins and effects of a 2D perspective that builds a platform to enter into a 3D reality. The next 3 numbers (4, 5, and 6) are the creative constructs holding the building properties for evolving the physical 3D plane. The final 3 numbers create relationship with qualities of mind and higher dimensions. Each dimension can be mastered by rising to the next level, because another energetic component is available. We can better understand 2D because we exist in a 3D world. As we raise consciousness to incorporate access to the fourth and fifth dimensions, we will attain greater mastery over our 3D experience. Expanding into higher dimensions gives us broader perspective and clarity since each level lends its unique energy and is inclusive of the dimension beneath it. As 3rd dimensional beings we can oversee a 2- dimensional reality and discern the difference between a square and a triangle. A 2-dimensional being existing on the same level would only see lines with no sense of what may lie behind them. Our elevated 3rd dimensional perspective offers us the ability to see deeper into the reality of 2D.

ANCIENT CULTURES UNDERSTOOD SACRED GEOMETRY

Ancient cultures had a deep understanding of Sacred Geometry and incorporated it into their architecture, art, religion, and philosophy. They achieved mastery over the 3D realm from their ability to interact with higher dimensional intelligence. Many of their concepts and buildings display a highly evolved understanding that mystifies us. Civilizations in ancient Egypt deeply respected wisdom beyond the material plane and used it to guide their lives.

Ancient temples were designed to be portals of energy. They had an enormous effect on people supporting their access to these higher realms. Structures built with Sacred Geometric designs and principles hold vibrational energy that transfers to people that consciously interact with them. They become conduits and antennae for higher dimensional access. Temples, cathedrals, mosques, and pyramids supported people to journey into higher levels of connection and awareness. This secret knowledge was held in high esteem throughout the ages.

However, history shows how advanced civilizations entered times of great challenge and darkness. Higher knowledge, intelligence, and creativity threatened rulers that wanted to control populations. Religions, conquerors, and governments determined this wisdom was an enemy. Knowledge went underground and was held by people like the Rosicrucians, Templars, Masons, and those who held mystical information. Sacred Geometry was built into the foundation and architecture of cathedrals in their design with few people understanding the impact it held. The potential and energy were laying low, waiting for the right time to resurface.

Sacred Geometry has so much to offer us now, and it's important to incorporate the powerful energetic aspects that three-dimensional Sacred Geometry structures offer to us. Our modern lifestyle is often a great distraction to the essential connections we need for health and well-being. Consciously connecting with the frequencies of higher dimensions offers the balance and stimulation that is an essential part of the evolutionary cycle we are part of.

UNDERSTANDING 2D VS 3D

While 2D drawings of Sacred Geometry are beautiful and inspiring, 3D Sacred Geometry significantly broadens the experience with tangible vibrational energy. These three-dimensional structures aligned with universal archetypes can transmit those same higher vibrational energies to our bodies, consciousness, and environment.

At Metaforms, we have conducted numerous scientific studies, including double-blind tests with subjects unaware of whether a geometric form is present or not. With the proper geometry hidden inside a box, a person's physiology and brain waves shift when it is hung above or near them.

People are often startled when they feel energy moving through one of our Sacred Geometry forms since it's not what they expected or were taught to believe. However, once we open to that possibility it feels natural and expansive. It's exciting to share the archetypal forms that we've experienced as conduits to higher dimensions, because on deep levels many people recognize and have worked with these universal principles.

Perhaps this is why so many people are attracted to Metatron's Cube as the 2D drawing with the 13 circles in the background marking the junction points on the pattern. It is at the forefront of powerful 3D forms that have been hidden for eons in plain sight. Even today, when you google "Metatron's Cube" over 99 percent of what you see is the 2D version. Let's now look at how it is created in 3D, the reality we inhabit.

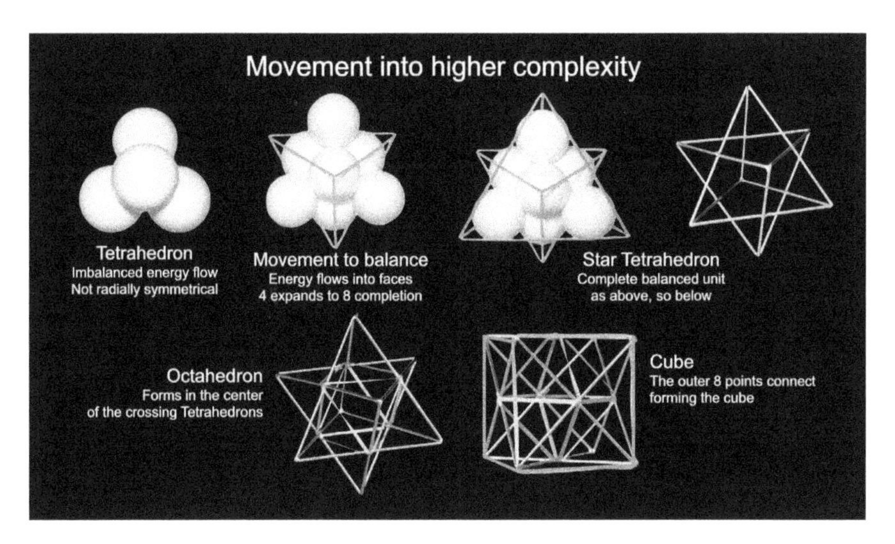

Fig. 8-1

In Fig. 8-1 you see the first 4 units (balls) coming together to create a tetrahedron. Unlike all the other platonic solids where faces are opposite faces and points are opposite points, the tetrahedron has 4 points opposite its 4 faces. Faces collect energy and points dissipate the energy. This means the tetrahedron is always pulling energy in from one face and dispersing it out the other side through the opposite point. Because of this strong, energy flow we recommend that by itself a tetrahedron is not used for energy work or to meditate within as a large pyramid, because it's never in stable equilibrium.

The Universe loves balance, so in the middle of each face a point grows opposite the first point. In Fig. 8-1 a ball is placed in the center of each face. Again, the tightest packing of spheres creates a balanced form now with 8 opposing points. Number 8 completes the field, introducing the fundamental building block of creation, a Star Tetrahedron with 1 tetrahedron pointing up and the other pointing downward. There are 6 places where the tetrahedrons cross each other. Connecting these 6 cross points to each other forms an octahedron in the center. Energy flows off the 8 points of the interlocking tetrahedrons. These outer 8 points connect, forming a cube. These 3 platonic solids come together in a nested fashion that is known as Metatron's Cube. It reflects how the physical aspects of Universe interact, creating a grounded flow of order and manifestation.

During the dark ages, while Europe was struggling to survive, Islamic scholars translated the works of Greek philosophers and kept the mathematical knowledge of the ancients alive. Unlike Christians who venerated iconic images of Jesus and the saints, the Islamic culture reflected their praise of Allah through beautiful calligraphy and geometric patterns. Their mosques were well known for their intricate tiling of two-dimensional designs.

These Islamic scholars used a process called orthogonal projection to translate three-dimensional forms into two-dimensional patterns. It's accomplished by shining a light through a geometric form onto a light background at a 90° angle to the light flow. We've seen a duplicate of the 2D Metatron's Cube in a book called *Islamic Patterns* by Keith Critchlow,[10] where they were representing the nesting of an octahedron and tetrahedron inside a cube. They used the hexagonal projection of the grouping because it was the best choice for tiling.

Leonardo Fibonacci was an Italian mathematician who studied with an Arab master when his father was the economic consul in Algeria. Leonardo brought the pattern of the nested solids back to Europe along with the Arabic numbering system of 1-9 plus zero in the early 1200s. He's best known for the numerical series named after him (the Fibonacci series) that works with the phi ratio (as we discussed in Chapter 7).

In the 1980s, the nested solids pattern was resurrected as a mystical symbol that generated all the platonic solids. That misconception persisted because all the platonic solids have one perspective where they will fit within a hexagon. (Fig. 8-2) The 3 forms that make up Metatron's Cube can accurately be traced, using the points found on the 2D projection, but the icosahedron and dodecahedron would be distorted from their true perspective if these same points are used.

---

10 Keith Critchlow, *Islamic Patterns: An Analytical and Cosmological Approach* (New York: W. W. Norton & Company, 1983).

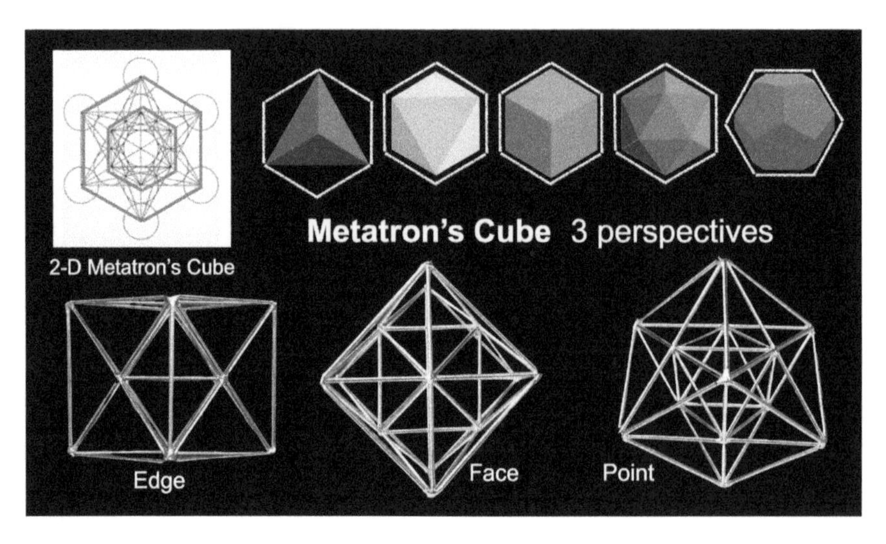

Fig. 8-2

More importantly, it takes at least three perspectives to gain enough information to build a three-dimensional form. This is the reason house plans give us the X and Y coordinates as a floor plan and the Z (third view) coordinate as the elevations. In the lower half of Fig. 8-2 are the 3 projections of Metatron's Cube. Each view has a different geometry and works with unique square roots, but all three are needed information in 2D if we are to be successful in creating the 3D structure they represent. Most 2D forms we see are meant to be 2D and are instructional and inspirational guideposts pointing our consciousness toward greater fields of understanding. However, they are not capable of moving higher dimensional energy. The reason is that 2-dimensional images and words exist only within our mind's perceptive awareness. If you turn the page they are printed on sideways, they disappear. They have no substance or power in our 3D reality except for what we give them – the placebo effect.

In this regard, frequently used 2D images can interact with our 3D reality by holding lower thought forms capable of introducing shifts in observers. The power to create interactions with higher dimensions still eludes them unassisted.

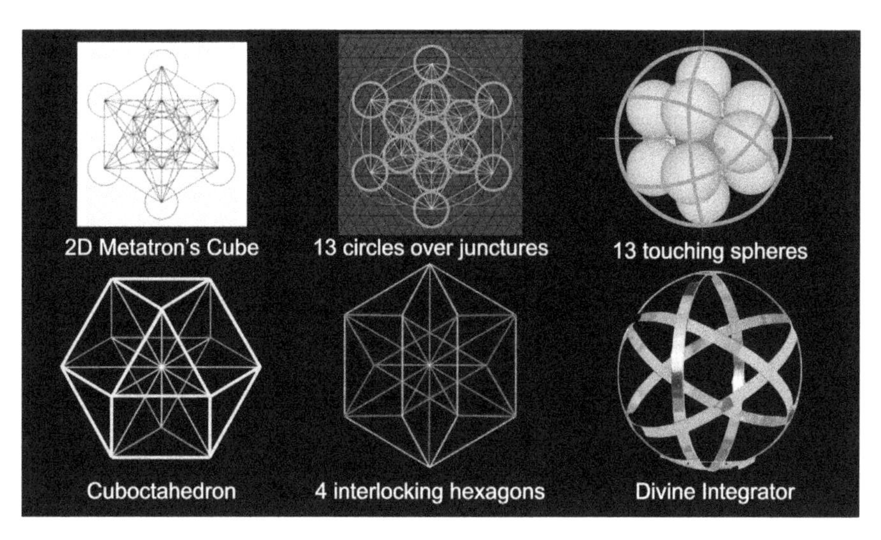

Fig. 8-3

If the 13 circles (Fig. 8-3) reflecting the junctures and structure of the 2D Metatron's Cube pattern are turned into spheres, a 3D form can be made. 3D patterns often differ greatly from their 2D counterparts partially because of gravity and attraction. With these governing aspects, the closest packing of 12 spheres is grouped around the 13th. Connecting the spheres reveals a form called a cuboctahedron made from 6 squares of a cube and the 8 triangles from an octahedron.

In the lower middle of Fig. 8-3, we've emphasized the outside lines forming 4 interlocking hexagons. When we transform the hexagons into circles, we get the form we've already shared when speaking of the 4 pillars of the sky in Chapter 4 – the Divine Integrator.

In fig. 8-4 are two gold images of Metatron's Cube that we have created in gold-plated bronze. One view toward the face and the other toward the point—both are orthogonal (right angle) projections. The white forms, generated by sound frequencies, are called Cymatics images by Hans Jenny. He was a medical doctor and his work on the effects of sound on matter was published in the 1960s. He created images using fluids and powders on flat plates that had different frequencies run through them generating the forms that you see here.

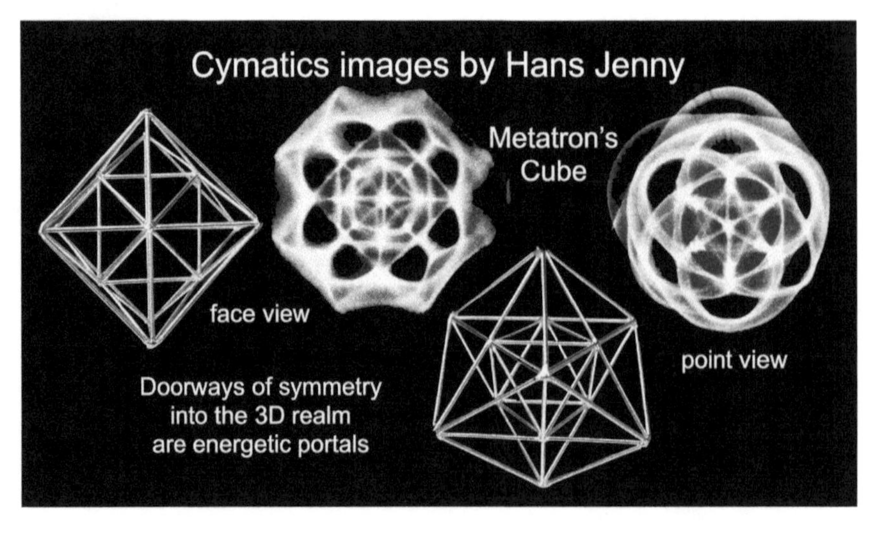

Fig. 8-4

These images were observed in a vibrating drop of water. Analyzing them offers several powerful insights. When the frequencies are changed, the patterns shown with Cymatics shift, and we witness two completely different images. When we realize that the two images are different perspectives of the same 3D geometry it becomes evident that sound is three dimensional, and we are witnessing a perspective shift of a 3D singularity (Metatron's Cube). What is shown with Cymatics is more than "change the frequency and change the pattern"; it shows that changing the frequency can shift the perspective within our 3D reality and each of these perspectives is linked to a different energetic frequency.

It further indicates that the orthogonal (right angle) projections of Metatron's Cube are archetypal and exist as pure energy that can be accessed through different mediums. This shows that every 3D geometry has at least 3 projections of perfect symmetry. Each of these directions in the 3D geometry offers a different portal of energy. Some directions are more helpful and beneficial than others. The point view of Metatron's Cube, for example, is the most active direction for moving energy.

Since a frequency (energy input) was used to generate these images, it leads us to understand that the solid forms of Metatron's Cube are reflections of pure energy movement. This energy is not an amorphous field but is organized and structured, following rules and patterns to replicate itself when stimulated by frequencies. This means that we can expect repeatable effects from the forms.

As we look closely at the Cymatics image of the point view, we can clearly see the energy flowing off the tips of the center star (octahedron) connecting to the next and then next form in the nested series. In an earlier chapter we described the flow of energy coming off the points of the tetrahedrons to connect to each other and create an outer cube. In this revealing image that flow of energy is clearly seen.

The energy that creates these Cymatics images does not reside in the white lines; rather, it exists within the dark spaces in between and forces the white powder or oil out of that area with its turbulence. Here's an analogy for a clearer understanding of what is being shared with that statement.

Imagine that you have a greenhouse room in your home near your kitchen. In between these two rooms is an old den that hasn't been used in years. You're busy and haven't cleaned it for a long time; however, many times a day you walk through to tend to your plants. After a while your movement through the room creates a clear path where you habitually walk. The dust and the dirt have moved toward the edges of the room. Energy is mysterious and invisible; we see its effects rather than the energy itself.

Energy is 99.99999 percent of our existence and matter is the null space or the densest and slowest aspects. It exists in the cracks of what is. The white Cymatics pattern that we see and relate to is where the energy isn't. For us to understand and work with reality we must identify and interact with what isn't here in the physical. To paraphrase Nikola Tesla—science needs to study non-physical phenomena.

Fig. 8-5

An exciting revelation occurs with applying the understanding that nothing is linear. If the energy of sound can structure reality, then the structure of reality can energize sound. We have demonstrated this with one of our tools called the Woven Spiral Star. (fig. 8-5) When words or sounds are spoken or played through this form, they shift and become fuller, more penetrating. The energy of the form couples with the energy of the sound moving it to a higher vibrational level. This heightened quality works over a distance and comes through in videos with the differences perceived and felt over a phone line and internet. Physical geometry can reinforce the geometry of sound to become a greater carrier of intent.

The platonic solids are important shapes in Sacred Geometry. There are only 5 solids that fit the criteria that all faces are the same in size and shape with all the angles and edges also being identical. They were named after the Greek philosopher Plato because he referenced them as the building blocks of creation in his well-known dialogue, *Timaeus* written in 360 BC. Pythagoras worked with them in 500 BC and stone sculptures of them have been found that were many thousands of years older. So how old are they?

In Fig. 8-6 we see some interesting mathematical addition. If we add up the total number of degrees found on the tetrahedron, octahedron, and dodecahedron and then multiply by 100 and convert to miles we get the diameter of the Sun. A different set of 4 solids gives us the exact diameter of the Earth, translating degrees into miles and the total of the cube equals the moon's diameter within 99.99 percent accuracy.

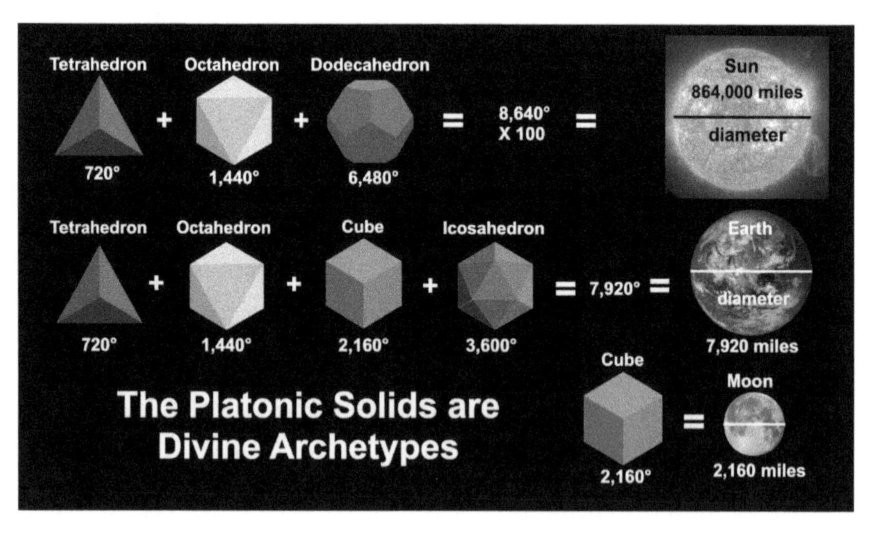

Fig. 8-6

This doesn't make sense to the rational, scientific perspective. The Universe shouldn't fit together like this, but it does. This is not speculation or some theory that must be proven. It simply is an observation of what is and it certainly gives more gravitas to the term "building blocks of creation". We are not arguing who or what did this, how or when or why it was done, but it is, and it has always been so.

These harmonic correlations only work if a degree is the exact measure that it is and 360 of them fit into a circle and a square. This only works if the mile is a divine measure that has been passed down from antiquity like many other hidden facts. The Romans named it the "mille" referencing a thousand paces, but they didn't invent it. The mile, the degree, and the platonic solids existed before creation. They are the components Universe uses to maintain order and coherence. They are archetypes, which are the structural aspects of creation that arise from consciousness. They are immutable and Universal in nature.

The amazing thing for us is experiencing the shifts in environments and human consciousness when these archetypes are grounded, solidified, and made tangible. When we take them out of the conceptual realm and build a physical analogue out of a conductive material the energy of the archetype starts pulsing through it in a way that most people can feel. As we've pointed out earlier, humanity has been creating an alternate reality with its technologies—a reality with its own frequencies and unnatural substances. This reality separates us from universal archetypes, from the reality of nature and from what is.

Our present technology is very powerful, but when we look at our planet, health, and culture, it's obvious that a rebalancing is greatly needed. We need a way of including the energies of universal archetypes into our technological growth so we can regain perspective and connect with the higher aspects of our humanity. Trying to block or hide from what we don't like never works, such as EMF-blocking amulets or stickers. This is old, separatist thinking. However, raising our vibrational level can counterbalance the technological effects that are distorting and lowering our energy field.

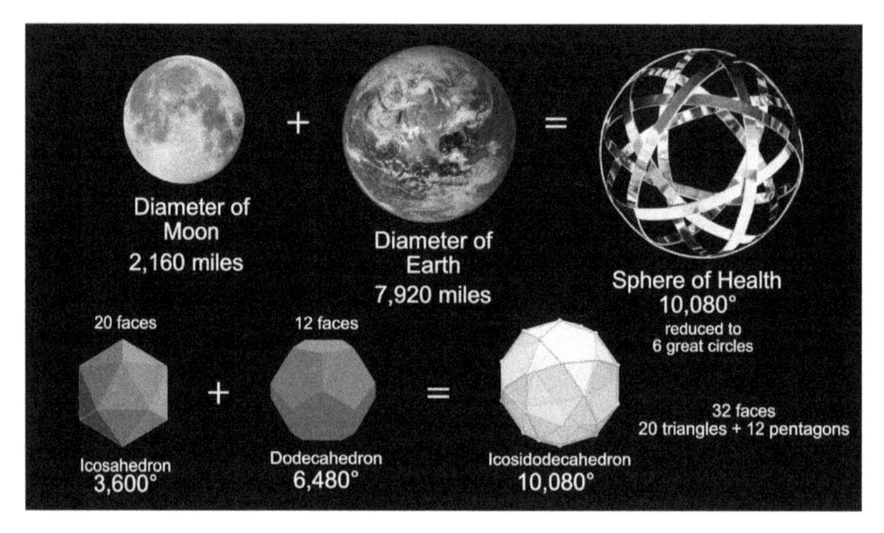

Fig. 8-7

Forms that resonate with higher archetypes appear in unexpected ways. (Fig. 8-7) Adding the diameter of the moon to the diameter of the earth gives us a total of 10,080 miles, which translates to the number of degrees in a form we call the Sphere of Health. It's also created by combining an icosahedron with a dodecahedron. The new form has the combined number of degrees and faces as its parents. The spherical projection brings in aspects of the feminine and the higher divine elements of the circle as there are 6 of them in the Sphere of Health. When the icosahedron interacts with the dodecahedron with the point of one fitting into the midface of the triangle or pentagon of the other they do so in the phi ratio. To fit together perfectly, the length of the icosahedron side is 1.618··· times the length of the dodecahedron side, forming phi ratio crosses. With the interaction of the moon and the Earth creating the same geometry it means they are actively supporting the phi ratio harmonic for the growth of all life on the planet.

The moon and the Earth continue this phi ratio dance in an amazing way as already shared in Fig. 6-10 of Chapter 6. If the moon and Earth were tangent to each other, a line drawn between their centers forms the long side of a right-angle triangle equal to 5,040 miles. The Earth's radius becomes the base and the length of the hypotenuse from the edge of the equator back to the center of the moon, discovered using the Pythagorean theorem: a2 + b2 = c2. Dividing the hypotenuse c by the Earth's radius equals 1.618···, phi. This is not something that happens easily by chance. It is a profound statement of perfection and engages in this universal play. Life has been following the divine harmonic of phi since the beginning of creation.

To carry on further with the unique number 5,040 presented by the combined radii of the Earth and moon, we find that it is the total product of the first seven numbers: 7! (known to mathematicians as factorial 7), and it is also the product of the last four numbers of the Decad (one through ten):

$$1 \times 2 \times 3 \times 4 \times 5 \times 6 \times 7 = 5040 = 7 \times 8 \times 9 \times 10$$

Exploring further with the unique relationship between the Earth and the moon we discover the solution to an ancient mathematical dilemma: the squaring of the circle where either the perimeters or areas of a square and circle are equal. Again, returning to the 2 orbs being tangent, we draw a circle centered on the earth whose edge passes through the center of the moon. We then construct a square surrounding the earth with each side equal to earth's diameter of 7,920 miles, for a total perimeter of 31,680 miles. Using the radius of the combined pair as 5,040 miles in the formula for the circumference of a circle ($C = 2\pi r$), we find that the circle passing through the center of the moon that is surrounding the earth equals the same 31,680 miles.[11]

Looking at the creation story in the Bible, we open to God in Genesis creating everything in 7 days. This is a sacred number that manifests itself as more than a quantity, for when we translate 7 days onto minutes (10,080), we arrive at the diameter of the Earth plus the diameter of the moon added together in miles. We've returned to the same number (10,080) and the same geometry displaying the phi ratio (Sphere of Health) embedded in sacred scripture. And there is more, for God begins their creation with light and as we'll discover this has a very profound connection to understanding and drawing together all our sacred numbers defining time and space.

The first day begins with light, but the light that we see is only .0035 percent of the entire spectrum of energy of which light is a part. The electromagnetic spectrum is a way of organizing all

---

11 John Michell with Allan Brown, *How the World Is Made: The Story of Creation According to Sacred Geometry* (Rochester, VT: Inner Traditions, 2012), page 22.

the different types of electromagnetic energy according to their wavelength and frequency. It includes radio waves, microwaves, infrared radiation, visible light, ultraviolet radiation, X-rays, and gamma rays. For our purpose we can use light as the generic container for all this energy because it is the component we can most easily relate to with our senses.

> **The geometry of light is the foundation wave-particle for the platonic solids and all of creation.**

All these different energy aspects have the same carrier, which is a quantum wave-particle called a photon. In 2016, two Polish scientists created the first hologram of a single photon as seen on the left in Fig. 8-8. This is a side perspective of a Star Tetrahedron, which was brought to my attention by David Wilcock. Let's look at the harmonic relationships with space and time that demonstrate this geometry to be that of a photon.

- At the bottom of this image, we recognize that it has 8 points, a complete and balanced energy field. Each point is made of 3 equilateral triangles. Adding up all the degrees gives us a total of 4320°.
- The major source of light and photons in our solar system is the sun with a radius of 432,000 miles.
- The speed of a photon, which is a function of time, is 4322 = 186,624 mps (miles per second). This is very close to Einstein's prediction of 186,282 mps, which differs by only 0.2 percent.

- 4,320 multiplied by 6, the number defining our space/time continuum = 25,920. In years this is equal to the Great Year encompassing all the ages of the zodiac.

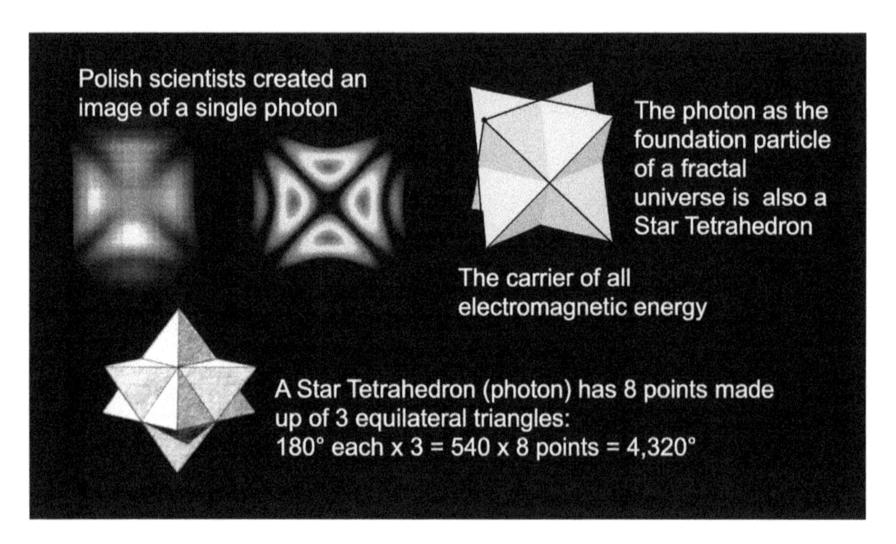

Fig. 8-8

The number 432 is a highly composite number, which means that it has many divisors. Some of the more significant harmonics manifest when 432 is divided by 4, it equals 108; by 6 = 72; by 12 = 36. Viewing these numbers as degrees gives us the angles for the two essential phi ratio triangles describing life and growth. This means that the phi ratio and life is a direct harmonic of light and the energy spectrum. The radically new concept that we are introducing here is that light and the energy spectrum carried by the photon has a geometry that we can relate to and use. We can use it by incorporating resonant aspects of the Star Tetrahedron and its 4320° as well as other geometries and patterns that are connected to it through harmonic resonance.

We've already seen how the Star Tetrahedron established itself as the first balanced geometry in creation growing out of the first form a tetrahedron. It immediately displays the first 3 platonic solids: the tetrahedron, octahedron, and cube. This initial grouping has come to be known as Metatron's Cube. Its energy along with these 3 platonic solids are focused on the physical dimension. Ancient philosophers were very interested in the higher realms and "how" the access through resonance was achieved. This important information was hidden in ancient scriptures and buildings as a record from the distant past.

The *Sefer Yetzirah* is "the oldest and most mysterious of all Kabbalistic texts."[12] It opens with this sentence: "With 32 mystical paths of Wisdom engraved Yah." This book and others explain that this first sentence is referencing the Hebrew Tree of Life with its 10 Sefirot and its 22 connecting pathways representing the 22 letters of the Hebrew alphabet. It is also referenced by the 32 times God's name is found in Genesis, the first book of the Bible.

A very powerful archetype stands behind 32, but to find it we must let go of the "things" associated with the number. The nouns and concepts are physical things that are just place holders. A true archetype is an energy flow and an operating principle with harmonic aspects that govern the creation of all that is. We can begin by looking at how consciousness creates and moves energy with 32, and toward the end of this chapter we will show how the builders of the Giza pyramid used it as well.

Expanding beyond the cube follows the same base harmonic of life that is resonating with our moon and earth, the phi ratio.

---

12 Aryeh Kaplan, *Sefer Yetzirah, The Book of Creation: In Theory and Practice* (San Francisco: Red Wheel/Weiser, LLC, 1997).

To discover this angle of growth we can create a phi ratio rectangle whose length divided by the width = 1.618···, phi. A diagonal drawn from one corner to the other gives us the smaller angle of 32°. This number is also a harmonic of Source beginning with 1 and expanding by multiples of two: 1 – 2 – 4 – 8 -16 – 32 – 64.

We call it the angle of enlightenment, 32° defines the difference between the physical dimension embodied by the cube and the higher etheric realms represented by the dodecahedron. In Fig. 8-9 we see small roof-like structures placed on top of each of the square cube faces. The large sloping part of each roof top forms an angle of 32° with the face of the cube. This is the important angle rising from the physical that creates higher dimensional access. Note that the roof tops alternate directions from one face to another. The long side has 3 lines contiguous to the bottom edge and the short side of the roof has 2. When all the roof top lines are connected, we have the 12 pentagonal faces of the dodecahedron.

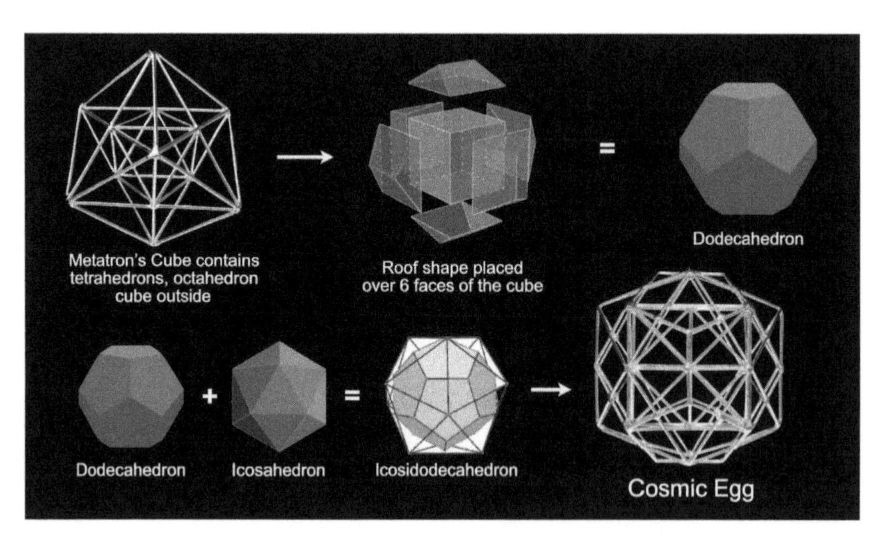

Fig. 8-9

The platonic solid that interpenetrates the dodecahedron (its dual) with the edge of one crossing over the edge of the other is the 20-sided icosahedron. The cross of the 2 sides is in a phi ratio relationship and the total number of sides between the two is 32. It is also the number of faces on the Sphere of Health, which works with the phi ratio and has the same number of degrees as the diameter of the earth plus the moon in miles – 10,080°.

The five platonic solids come together in a single form we call the Cosmic Egg. The icosahedron on the outside of the form can rest inside an octahedron, dividing each arm into a phi ratio relationship where one of the icosahedron's twelve points touch one of the twelve arms making up the octahedron. This new octahedron surrounding the icosahedron is the same platonic solid found at the core of this progression of geometries, which means this entire progression can endlessly repeat itself as a 3D fractal, with the Star Tetrahedron being the seed. This shows that the geometry of light is the foundation wave-particle for the platonic solids and all of creation.

Much of the information coming down to us through fable and myth originated from survivors of the world deluge over 11,600 years ago. They had developed a multi-dimensional technology that allowed them to cut and move blocks of stone over a thousand tons each. Evidence of their existence has been steadily mounting; however, our interest is in deciphering the ancient clues to see what they teach us about Sacred Geometry. The first steps in progressing from abstract mental images is to find its meaning with actual geometries by ascribing degrees to the numbers to discover what they build.

THE HARMONICS OF ENERGY

The examples that follow point toward an understanding of the harmonics of energy based on the geometry of a photon being a Star Tetrahedron. An ancient Norse myth offers us the story of a final battle of the gods attempting to restore order:

> **500 doors and 40 there are**
> **I ween, in Valhalla's walls:**
> **800 fighters through each door fare,**
> **When to war with the Wolf they go**

The Star Tetrahedron (photon) has 8 points that are passageways for energy flow and the number of degrees in each one is 540°. The total of the 8 points is 4320°. The math from the Norse myth is equal to the radius of the sun at 432,000 miles (540 × 800).

From ancient India comes a 4,000-year-old Vedic scripture called the Rig Veda. It has 10,800 stanzas with each one composed of 40 syllables. Researchers have also found that the number of bricks in the sacred Indian fire-altar equals 10,800. In the Rig Veda, if the 10,800 stanzas are multiplied by the 40 syllables in each one, we get a total of 432,000. When translated to miles we have the radius of the Sun and with two fewer zeros, the photon as a Star Tetrahedron appears with 4320°.

What is so special about 10,800 that it shows up in these different places? The usual sacred number that is referenced is

108, and we've shared many of those examples. It seems like a lot of extra work for both the authors of the Rig Veda and the fire altar builders to use a number as large as 10,800 without a significant reason.

We looked for geometries that would fit this larger value. If we reduce the size of the sun's diameter by two magnitudes (removing two zeros) to 8,640 miles and add it to the moon's diameter of 2,160 miles, we have 10,800 miles. The moon plus the sun offers us the special harmonic resonance that was possibly encoded in this ancient scripture and holy fire-altar.

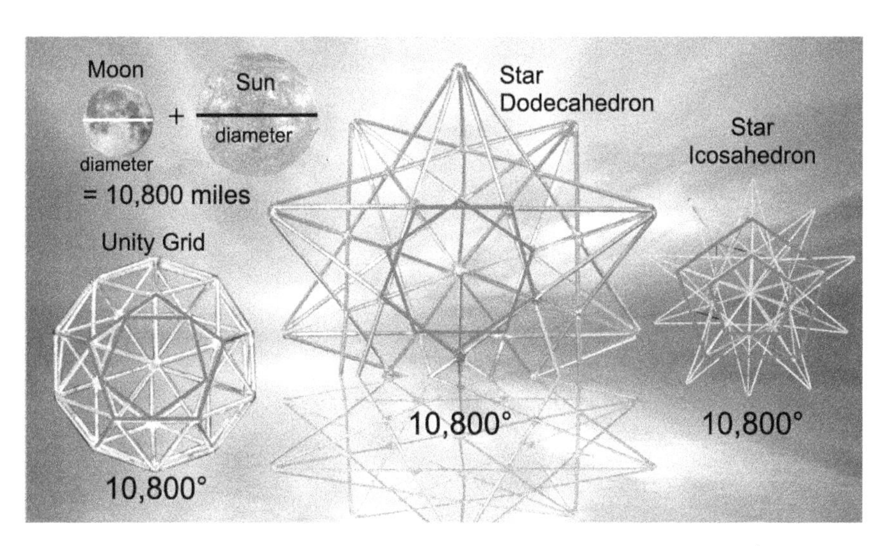

Fig. 8-10

However, could there also be a geometry connected with this number that is harmonically resonant? As it turns out there are 3 geometries that fit the parameters. As you can see in Fig. 8-10 the

Star Dodecahedron and Star Icosahedron are platonic solids that we're familiar with and these 2 have points added to each face. These points are created from golden phi ratio triangles creating 5-sided pyramids on the dodecahedron and 3-sided pyramids on the icosahedron. By connecting the tips of the pyramids on the dodecahedron, we get an icosahedron and connecting the icosahedrons tips gives us a dodecahedron. This is the way these 2 forms move back and forth, one transforming into the other, through their pyramidal points in a dance that moves toward infinity.

The third geometry forms a sphere of 60 triangles with each triangle equal to the faces on the great Pyramid at Giza. It's called the Unity Grid, and we've overlaid it and the other forms with pentagons, which have 108° angles to demonstrate their relationship with the golden phi ratio. These geometries are the harmonics of growth referenced by the Rig Veda with all three being resonant with the moon and the sun.

The most impressive confirmation of the importance of 432 comes from a new interpretation of the measurements used by the large Giza pyramid. Today, there are many researchers expressing a belief that the Giza pyramid is much older than currently believed, perhaps tens of thousands of years older. Regardless of age, here are two perspectives I would like to present for a new understanding of some essential facts.

- The builders had precise understanding of what they were building including all the fine details that we are still discovering today. It was all intentional.

- It was not built as a tomb, but was constructed with the intent of working with energy. There have been many studies on the energies generated by the pyramid shape alone, so when I heard again the following facts on the Giza pyramid's measurements, they struck me in a new and more enlightened way.

As seen in Fig. 8-11, researchers started with a model of the moon touching the surface of the Earth, as we addressed earlier in this chapter, and then overlayed a cross-section of the pyramid with its tip on the moon's center and its base resting exactly on the equator. When this was done the base length of the pyramid equaled the diameter of the earth. The researchers then discovered that fitting the Giza pyramid within the planet's profile such that the height was equal to the polar radius of the earth would create a relationship such that the perimeter of the resized pyramid would equal the circumference of the earth. The scale that was used to create both relationships is 1:43,200.

They could have made their pyramid smaller or larger using a different scale. They were totally free to choose whatever scale they wanted, and they chose this one which is a harmonic of the base fundamental of the energy spectrum that can reinforce the energetic flow they were seeking that perfectly relates to the Earth's essential measurements of diameter and circumference. The Sun and the photons it produce resonate with 432. The ancient builders realized that harmonizing with light is a key to enhancing energy flow.

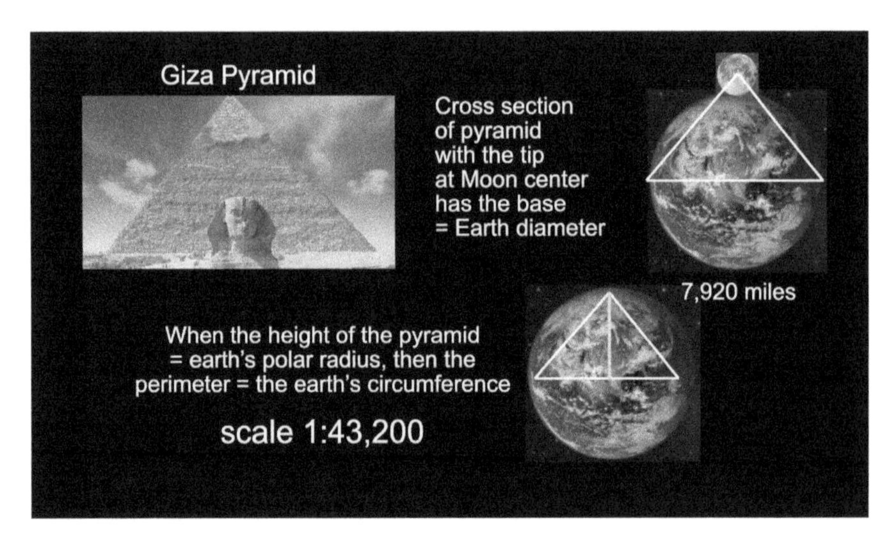

Fig. 8-11

It's amazing how the cross-section of the pyramid aligns with the Earth, however that seems to be one of the only sets of measures that researchers have focused on. There are books with the authors marveling at how the ancient builders managed to produce such a precise interior slope angle of 51.85°. However, they didn't. They were not building to create this angle at all. It's simply what showed up as they were focusing on something more important—the face of the pyramid. The face is where the energy is collected, and its angles are what matter. Remember the angular totals of the different platonic solids totaling the diameters of the sun, moon, and Earth? Those were face values that were used and those are the angles referenced in all our comparisons.

For example, we could cut an octahedron in half, and it would look like a square-based pyramid. It was easily and directly made by using 4 equilateral triangles all having angles of 60°. When we sit it on the earth and measure the inside slope angle, that is a more complicated measure equaling 54.73°. The internal slope angle was not our focus, the outside equilateral triangles were our focus.

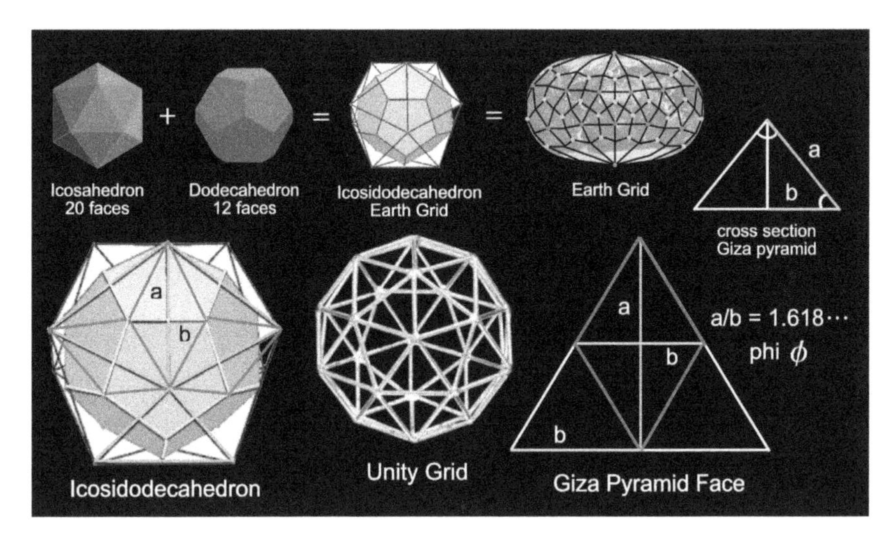

Fig. 8-12

The ancient builders created the face of the Giza pyramid based on a triangle with an internal relationship to the phi ratio, where the height is divided by half the base. Its base angles are each 58.28° leaving a peak angle of 63.43°. We can recreate this triangular face several ways. In Fig. 8-12 we see the example of a dodecahedron and icosahedron interpenetrating each other creating a diamond shape where the long center line of the icosahedron edge is crossed by the edge of the dodecahedron. Dividing the long edge by the short edge of the dodecahedron equals 1.618···. Cutting the diamond in half along the short edge gives us 2 triangles equal to the faces of the Giza pyramid.

On the right side of Fig. 8-12, we've subdivided the pyramid face into 4 smaller versions of the whole face with the middle triangle pointing downward. The smaller triangles maintain the same proportions and angles as the whole triangular face. Half the base has been given the value of one, which is equal to the interior cross section's value of one. The outside slope of the cross section that equals Φ (phi) is the same length as the height of the outer triangular face of the pyramid. The height of the face of the Giza pyramid divided by half the base is equal to phi – Φ – 1.618···. The Unity Grid in the middle is made from sixty triangular faces that all share the same dimensions as the faces of the Giza pyramid.

The capstone of the pyramid displays another important geometric relationship. It's here that the number 32 found in the beginning lines of the *Sefer Yetzirah* reveals its value as the ascension angle. During World War II, a plane flew over the great pyramid at the right time of day that emphasized the shadows cast, showing each face precisely split down the middle with a slight indentation that made them concave. What was originally thought to be a 4-sided pyramid is 8-sided with the peak angles split in 2. Number 8 is the playing field necessary for maximum effect and the capstone is the strongest outflow of energy for the pyramid. Each of these newly discovered angles is 32° (31.72°), the ascension angle employed by the pyramid builders to generate the higher dimensional access they sought.

TAKE A MOMENT TO REFLECT . . .

We've taken you on a journey to learn how geometry and numbers are filled with clues to understand Universe and ourselves. Discovering these geometric patterns and cycles awakens the wisdom within to restore inner knowing and essential connections to all that is.

We find meaning and purpose in our relationship with our origin. Learning our biological family tree strengthens human foundation and satisfies the need to feel connected. We are a species that longs to overcome loneliness and feel true belonging. Numbers, angles, and their related geometries express the story of creation so we can evolve to higher capability.

The Universe is an abundant and loving system that constantly displays its ingenious and unlimited potential. As we understand and respect the principles of creation, we open our hearts and minds to become divine co-creators that work together for the good of all. It is through resonance that consciousness directs the creative force to manifest a life for the good of all. Breathe this energy into your heart. Allow yourself to expand into the unity and magnificence of a fully present, soul-centered life. Your feelings, intents, thoughts, and actions give rise to your growth and the evolution of this Universe.

Imagine what each moment feels like when pure love is your highest intention. That influence is the basis of creation and miracles happen by aligning with this energy, impressing life with compassion and joy.

Through staying connected, we trust our relationship with Source and everything around us. Our consciousness molds how this Universe evolves. We are more than receivers; we are the rhythm that defines creation.

CHAPTER 9
USING SACRED GEOMETRY TO TRANSFORM YOUR LIFE

Since the early 1980s we have been aware of the powerful effects that Sacred Geometry offers to us and our environment. In 1985 when we met, we recognized we had a mission to create beautiful tools and contribute to raising consciousness on the planet.

We have applied the knowledge shared in this book to our pendants and various structures. We've been delighted with the value it's offered to many thousands all over the world. We've found people are naturally attracted to what we've created because it's based upon universal principles and when worn, or placed in your home or office, the profound sense of connection we hunger for supports all aspects of our lives.

All our technology works with the 3-dimensional qualities of geometry simply because we live in a 3-dimensional system and our physical body interacts with this and higher planes of existence. Many people are familiar with 2-dimensional Sacred Geometry images that are quite beautiful and inspiring. However, as we shared earlier, flat images are translated inside our brain, and don't exist outside of the mind's ability to interpret these images. It's your interaction that gives them meaning and stimulates the energy you may feel. The movement of physical energy requires a 3D antenna system to interact with and 2D doesn't have that energetic presence in our dimension. If 2D images did transfer energy on their own in our dimension, then one could feel energy radiating from books that contain hundreds of drawings. We've conducted double blind tests where unseen 3D forms engender an immediate response on brain wave, EEG equipment.

In 2002, we began exploring how to get the full impact of our sacred geometric tools into a small pendant that could be worn all the time. We realized that 2-dimensional patterns did not interact with our reality in the same way as the three-dimensional structures we were building that aligned with a full energetic flow. We finally discovered there was a way we could build a 2-dimensional antenna system that would create a multidimensional energy flow laying a pathway into the dimensions of Soul and higher consciousness.

In the last chapter we spoke of needing 3 different perspectives to build a house or any 3D object. The points outlining a 3D form need to be defined on an X, Y, and Z axis. When we look at 3D geometries that fit inside a sphere there are at least 3 perspectives where the sun shining through them casts a shadow forming a beautiful, symmetrical pattern. The main 3 projections are through a point, a face, and an edge. We chose the sun because the light needs to be far enough away so that its rays are parallel to each other, which allows the back side of the geometry to collapse into the front without distortion. As we've shared before, the generated image/shadow is at a right angle to the rays of light, and is referred to as an orthogonal projection. With this concept in mind, we can accomplish the same thing mathematically without the need for an actual light projection.

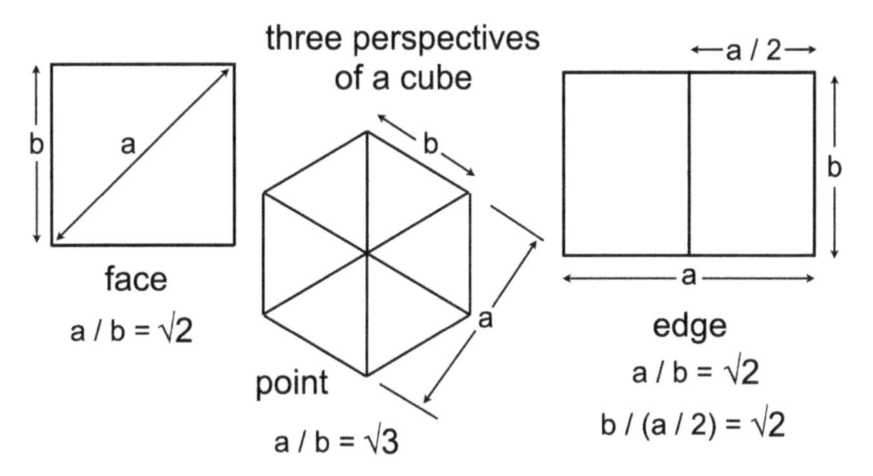

Fig. 9-1

In Fig. 9-1 We're sharing these concepts with a geometry, the cube, that will be one of the simplest for the reader to visualize. With the face view you can understand the importance of parallel flows of light collapsing the back side of the geometry into the front with all the extra lines hidden behind the face. Looking at the edge gives us a large rectangle divided into two smaller rectangles of equal dimensions. This is a distortion from the original cube, which is composed of 12 equal sides.

In every case when a geometry is orthogonally projected it distorts into a symmetrical mandala based on one of the major square roots: $\sqrt{2}$; $\sqrt{3}$; $(\sqrt{5}+1) / 2$ = Phi. In the edge view of the cube, the length of the long side divided by the short side of each of the three rectangles = 1.414···, $\sqrt{2}$. The diagonal of the face divided by the side length also = $\sqrt{2}$.

Shifting one's perspective to the view toward the point (vertex, corner) a completely different geometry emerges. In this view the distance between opposite sides of the hexagon divided by the length of a side = $\sqrt{3}$, 1.732···.

We found that by building these 3 perspectives in a conductive material, we used gold-plated copper, on a non- conductive substrate like fiberglass, and then surrounding the images with a circle, we could attract 3D energies with a 2D antenna system. The circle creates a unity within its boundaries allowing the separate perspectives to take on the energetic qualities of the whole three-dimensional geometry. It's also important that the patterns have thickness allowing them to be an actual 3D pattern.

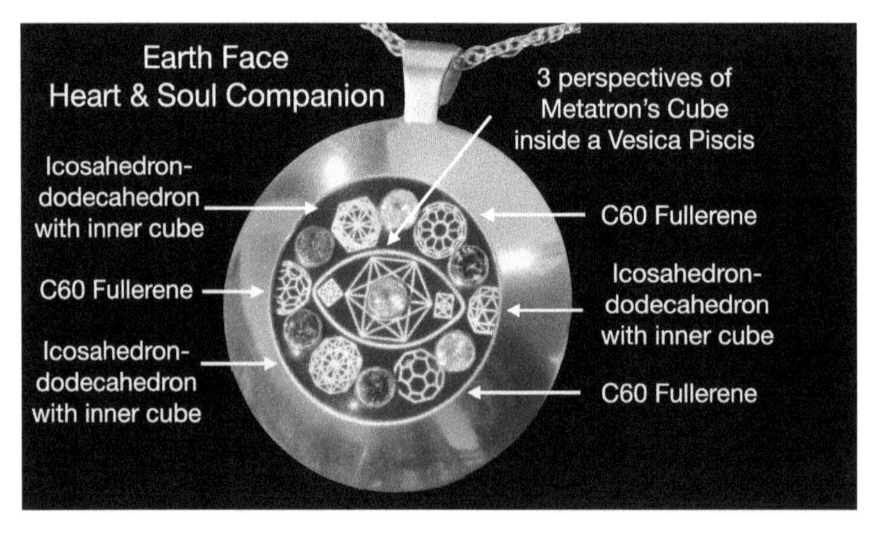

Fig. 9-2

Fig. 9-2 shows the earthside of the Heart & Soul Companion (a 2-sided energetic pendant) with 10 different geometric patterns. We've pointed out the three images to complete a C60 Fullerene molecule, another three create the energies of an icosahedron interpenetrating a dodecahedron with a cube at its center, and the third set offers Metatron's Cube in the center of a vesica piscis. We have different sets of geometric forms on the inside of the fiberglass plate and on both sides of the star face, which is on the other side of this 2-sided pendant.

By combining different geometric forms, we are able to affect the entire energetic field of the body when the pendant rests within a few inches of its surface (within the etheric body). With the earthside towards the body, the energy flows downward, creating a grounding sense of feeling connected to the body and to the earth. Turning the other side of the pendant (star face) toward the body shifts the energetic flow upward, stimulating mental focus and a more outward, energetic expression.

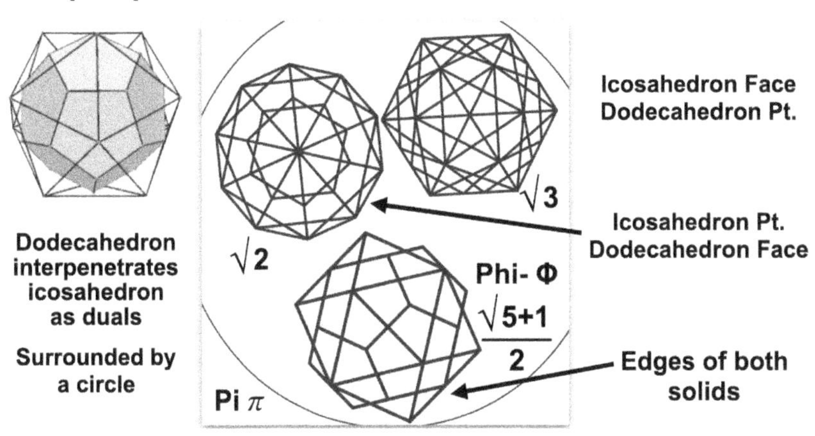

Fig. 9-3

In Fig. 9-3, we have the 3 perspectives of the face, edge, and point (orthogonal projections—right angle projections) of an

icosahedron/dodecahedron dual. Unique energy flows happen with each perspective separate from the synergistic whole they create together. Looking closely at each mandala, it becomes evident that the underlying geometries are completely different. If we were to choose points on each pattern that would allow us to construct rectangles with parallel sides, we would discover that the bottom pattern has Phi ratio rectangles, and the projection on the top right with a 6-pointed star in its center would have a rectangle where the long side divided by the short side equals the square root of 3. Each of these views is a different portal of energy, which becomes more important when working with 3D forms, as the energy shifts depending on the direction facing you. In the case of the pendant, all the square roots of creation are present from each form plus Pi, π, which comes in through the circular container.

In working with these higher dimensional flows of energy the body is at choice as to which energies to work with and which to ignore. What we refer to as subtle or higher energies underlie everything. This increases their flow and is like giving the body the space and support to realign with the divine blueprints that are innate within our being. This is a very different dynamic than working with strong physical substances like pharmaceutical drugs that give the body no choice but to succumb to the power of the drug and it frequently affects other parts of the body as well resulting in negative side effects.

Additionally, the pendants have dozens of internal antenna systems: circuit boards; frequency generators; a photon source; fiber optic and carbon fiber systems; 3 layers of different depositions of molecular geometries; 10 toroidal constructs; alchemical mixtures of 15 different crystals, chemicals and rare earth metals; orgone layering; antenna systems made with silver, gold, copper, and titanium; whole pearls, and kunzite spheres. Fitting all of this into a small space is a challenging process that involves peering through a binocular microscope to complete the finishing welds.

Fig. 9-4, Star Face and Earth Face of the Heart & Soul Companion Highlight pendant

The Heart & Soul Companion pendant is a beautiful transformative technology that is worn close to the heart for living a soul centered life. This 2-sided pendant displays Sacred Geometry faces adorned with high quality gemstones. The connections enhanced by the pendant offer greater mindfulness, reduce stress and lead to a life of greater joy, purpose, and well-being.

There are various styes that differ only by the gems that are on each face. The gems fulfill a vital role in energetically bridging the gap between the emotional and physical body. The energy of each chakra reflects the vibrational colors of the rainbow starting with red at the root chakra stimulated by red ruby and garnet to the violet radiance of the crown chakra activated by purple amethyst.

We've had so many people share their stories with us about how wearing the pendant has improved their lives from a short "wow" to occurrences of healing and profound life changes. The powerful shifts people have experienced over the years have touched us deeply. One favorite story is from a young man who was rather skeptical about making the purchase. His personal words are shared here.

> **I put my pendant on the moment I got it and what I felt immediately thereafter cannot be described in words. Growing up as a kid I always had a poor self-image, lack of confidence, and quite a bit of anxiety. However, for the first time in forever, I felt completely at peace. I felt like I was living in the "now" and not in the drudge of the past, or fear of the future. I felt a sense of personal well-being and elevated awareness I have never felt before. Meditation has taken on an unbelievable new level of relief for me, as before I felt like I struggled to find my "center" and release myself mentally of all**

thought. Now with my Heart Companion I drift into a heightened sense of awareness almost immediately. My sleep has improved astronomically, and that is something I have struggled with for most of my life. All of what I listed so far is just the tip of the iceberg, but it is the best I can put into words. It is like I am now not at the mercy of my emotions or somebody else's; I am free. I am the sole architect of my future now, and that's an incredible feeling. One of the most incredible changes I have yet to mention has to do with my career. I am a 911 dispatcher for a living for a very busy county here in Illinois and it goes without saying our job is extremely stressful. I work many long and odd hours, I am away from my family most of the time, and the stress from all the graphic incidents really take a toll on you. We are the first to hear the emergency, last to know— if ever—what happens. It's a tough job, no doubt, and that comes with the job I understand... but I would not be human if I said it did not wear on me to hear the bad and the ugly all day, every day, as nobody calls 911 because they are having a good day. With the iConnect initially, and now the Heart Companion, the toxicity of the environment cannot take a hold of me anymore. I see myself as an observer and an intricate part of something very important, and no longer feel powerless and worn out when I go home. I do not let anyone "into my temple" of sacred peace for lack of a better term that these magical tools have afforded me with. Also,

> **my sense of someone else's emotional state or mindset over the phone has increased significantly. It's like my inner intuition has skyrocketed and I'm very sensitive to the state of mind of those around me. Thank you thank you for this incredible tool; Enzo and my relationship alone has dramatically taken a turn in where we never, ever argue anymore, and we seem to be so in tune with one another like we never have been. This tool is crafting the peak of my life, and I owe you so much thanks for making this a reality for us.**
>
> ***—Anthony***

THE IMPORTANCE OF OUR LAND IN ENERGIZING

The hardware is only part of the process. How and where it is energized and connected to the Earth Grid evolves and completes the energy of the pendant using planet Earth as a receiver and broadcaster.

We live on 177 acres in a valley near Lyons, Colorado. The feng shui is perfect, with a river flowing from west to east in the south and a mountain close to 8,000 feet in the north. Feng shui arose from a Chinese practice of arranging pieces in living spaces to create balance with the natural world. Unique energy flows found in nature created by mountains, valleys, and rivers are valuable elements to determine the optimal places to build. These localized energy hotspots often coincide with the larger energy flows of ley lines, which crisscross the earth like the nervous system of the planet. Many of the important churches and sacred sites in Europe were built on ley lines of energy. The churches often found the exact locations by building over the top of a pagan site that may have existed for thousands of years. What we have learned from our guidance is that mountains can draw up and focus earth energy like a pyramid. An important understanding of this process of working with guidance is that it is an aspect of us, unlike opening a book or receiving a lecture. It is discovery, experimentation, discernment, and being responsible for our choices. Guidance allows our ego to be engaged, useful, and, most of all playful. The situation is like a parent watching a young child with a coloring book. They don't step in offering to do the coloring because they know how it "should" be done. The growth and engagement of the child is the focus. Although guides can offer fertile environments until the discoveries needed for the next step arrive. This way we can be open to the bookthat falls off the shelf.

Our revelations on mountains were catalyzed by a trip in 1995 to the palace of Knossos on the island of Crete. Originally built over 4,000 years ago, this multistory structure was huge, with many rooms unlike anything else from that time. The advanced complexity of their palace, combined with their worship of the bull, gave rise to the myth of the labyrinth and the minotaur, who was half bull and half man. Bulls were inserted into the myth because the ancient Minoans performed acrobatic dances with bulls during their spring rituals and worked with the horns of a bull as a religious symbol.

There were many upright sculptures of horns six to eight feet high placed on pedestals around the palace. Many of them had the tips curved outward like upstretched hands of welcoming and the lines flowing downward curved gently toward a rounded base. They offered the appearance of a vase sliced in half and we realized that was indeed how they were being used: as receptacles. They had constructed vessels designed to catch energy that were all aligned with a double-peaked mountain in the distance. We were viewing an ancient display that had unique similarities to the geography of our land. The double-peaked mountains to the west of our home were facilitating the same energy flow!

Finding, procuring, and building on our land was a long and circuitous path that was directed by guidance. Acknowledging the help we receive keeps us on track with the correct understanding that is often put to the test. We've been able to streamline our progress of discovery over the traditional, time-consuming process of trial and error.

Fig. 9-5

We took this trip as we were in the process of buying our land in Colorado, and what was revealed in Crete opened us to the energy flows on our land where three double peaked mountains line up like the focus sights on a rifle barrel. What we have found is that these mountains catch and move energy within a specific broadcast angle emanating outward between the peaks. To the west of us, sitting on the continental divide at over 14,000 feet high are the double peaks of Long and Meeker (Fig. 9-5, top two images). Moving toward our land the energy is refocused and strengthened by the 11,500-foot-high mountain of Twin Sisters (upper left in front of Long's peak) before it connects to our twin-peaked mountain called Blue, which is one of the highest this far east in the Rocky Mountains (bottom two images with our home on the left).

In 2000, the year we moved into our home, there were a number of lightning strikes causing fires as large as 140 acres. I would be in my workshop and hear a loud thunderclap. Rushing outside, I saw blue sky everywhere except for one small black cloud at the base of the mountain with a thin plume of smoke rising from the top of the cliff. It was a very unsettling experience that was later smoothed over by our guidance explaining that they were using the lightning strikes to open portals on the mountain and activating the many vortexes on our land.

Our mountain has a large quartz outcropping between its peaks at its throat center, as seen on the lower right of Fig. 9-5. The year following the lightning strikes that occurred along the lower spine of Blue, there was a major strike squarely on the quartz outcropping near her peaks, igniting another fire, and activating the energy flow for the entire set of three mountains.

We've placed forms on Blue's peaks and built pyramids and geometries over many of the vortexes on our land to stabilize and balance them as they form a line of flowing energy directed to the main vortex where all the geometries and pendants are charged. After this, the energy is directed a short distance into an entrance point for the Earth Grid, which flows south along the front range of the Rockies through Colorado Springs, where Nikola Tesla took advantage of the energy flow to activate his large generators built in 1899. He worked with higher guidance and was very aware of the energy grid system of the planet accessed by the great pyramid at Giza and other sacred sites.

We and friends have buried crystal-laden forms all over the world at pivotal sites to enhance energy flows and connect to our land in Colorado through the Earth Grid system. Selling many thousands of sacred geometric forms worldwide has had a similar energizing and grid enhancing effect as their energy has enhanced the network. One of the primary connections began decades ago when we were told of our deep relationship with Uluru, in central Australia, which lies almost opposite us on the other side of the planet. Its activation with similar geometries as found on our land began a toroidal flow through the planet, blossoming out at both ends and surrounding earth.

As shown in Fig. 9-6 we have two chambers with stacks of forms spinning on Causal Generators, which are special motors we have built to precisely control the rotational speed of a geometry, which activates it by interplaying with time and the surrounding electromagnetic fields. These motors also generate special frequencies that enhance the energetic outreach of the geometries into higher dimensions. Many of the geometries spin inside large tubes wrapped with wires conducting frequencies that have been energetically enhanced and overlaid many times to increase their potency. While charging, the pendants are placed inside the energetically wrapped tubes.

Fig. 9-6

Both chambers are connected to large 15-foot forms anchored between them. Everything is directed into the Earth Grid via a vortex entry point nearby, and the chambers have been programed to automatically run for 24 hours every 72 hours (three days). Pulsing into the Earth Grid helps promote positive planetary shifts and stimulates us into accessing higher dimensional realms during sleep.

Many of the forms in the chambers are found on the pendant faces and their energy pulsing through the planetary grid keeps the energies supplied by the pendants continually high and activated. More importantly, a growing web of positive higher consciousness is being accessed. The energy coming to each person is vibrationally raised by the pendant and the energy emanating from each being is also raised. This was clearly demonstrated by a grandmother who said her grandchildren used to run away from her when she visited, but after wearing the pendant they started crawling all over her. This positive energy shift transforms every person's experience, and it also flows back into the connective Earth Grid for the good of all.

THE CHALLENGE OF MEASURING SUBTLE ENERGIES

It's an interesting riddle trying to use 3D technology to measure what isn't 3D, i.e., subtle energy. It doesn't work directly, but we can measure the changes in human physiology. Over the past 40 years, we've worked with many types of equipment with doctors conducting studies demonstrating that physical sacred geometric technology can change lives.

> *The significant increases in all of these tests show a dramatic effect of the Advanced I.Connect and Heart Companion to increase an individual's health and vitality. These results support the I.Connect claim, that when held on the body, energy flows and health improves.*
>
> ***– Lisa Tully, PhD***

We could also measure a person's energy field becoming stronger with all their internal organs becoming balanced. The shifts in the emotional body on the fourth-dimension and the mental body on the fifth are more difficult to understand as they are invisible to most of us.

Some people use aura cameras, but they cannot directly record those subtle bodies. They actually measure skin conductivity (galvanic skin response or electrodermal activity), which is a measure of our emotional arousal. One's emotional states are calculated through different algorithms and then projected onto an image of the person as a possible reflection of what could be happening in their aura.

We've used EEG equipment to measure the electrical activity of the brain and it has demonstrated that subjects sitting under certain geometries can be awake and involved in a focused task that would normally push them into the active range of beta brain waves, but they remain present and access information through a theta and delta range that are usually indicative of deep sleep. To us it reflects higher dimensional access during the waking state.

One of the more interesting responses came from a researcher who tested me while meditating with some of these tools and told me that my brain waves appeared similar to the images she saw when measuring a yogi while he was passing 10-inch needles through his body with no loss of blood or injury. To rise above bodily limitations, it makes sense that we must rise above this dimensional reality and enter higher dimensional realms—the abode of Spirit.

In the end, the most meaningful aspect is your personal experience. For this reason, I don't bring up the studies when talking to people, I just put a Heart & Soul Companion pendant in their hand and muscle test them. Applied kinesiology (muscle testing) is a method where I press down at the end of someone's extended arm and ask them to resist the pressure or be strong. This is simple and direct enough that anyone can learn to do it by themselves with finger resistance or with a friend using your extended arm for them to put pressure on. After thousands of tests with people, I've never seen it fail. Rarely, I get a macho person who is trying to prove that it doesn't work by overpowering me. I explain that I'm not arm wrestling him and it is simply feedback for him from his body. If we can leave our analytical mind out of the picture, the body can step forward and very accurately share what it needs by remaining strong for positive resonance or turning weak when something isn't supportive.

After asking someone to be strong, I press down on their wrist with a firm pressure. I ask them to state their name and then a made-up name, the difference in strength reflects how their body reacts to the truth or a lie. Lying always makes the body weaker as it disconnects us from the higher realms of our truth. I then measure weakness when I ask them to think of something that makes them unhappy, or I have them hold an active cell phone next to their head, or I put an artificial sweetener in their hand. In all cases, it is easy to push their arm down with only two of my extended fingers at their wrist because these are thoughts, energies, or toxins that disconnect them from a higher dimensional flow of energy. After each trial demonstrating weakness, I repeat the test with one of our pendants touching their body. In each case they become so strong that I can't move their arm down at all.

The reason for their increased strength is connection to the larger part of themselves, to higher self, to Source. They expand beyond the 10 percent that shows up in the physical realm and start to incorporate the bigger part of their being in a resonant dance of energetic flow activating and aligning many of their subtle bodies. Connection allows for the Source codes of creation to bring us into balance and strength. The negative effects of EMFs, toxins, and fear foster disconnection. The weaknesses and difficulties we measure in our 3D reality are the side effects of disconnection. Muscle testing is simply a mirror to this process, and as we experience connection more frequently its loss is easily recognized. Thoughts of separation, sadness, and fear become more and more distasteful.

When given a choice the physical and subtle bodies have a natural proclivity to align with the highest order available. When divine archetypes are physically introduced, they attract the high vibrations of creation and establish resonance to ground the higher flow for our benefit.

UNDERSTANDING GEOMETRIC TECHNOLOGY AS A TOOL

The Woven Spiral Star is a good example of how we can apply the information we've been discussing toward a practical tool.

First, however, we would like to explain our use of the word "tool." If we think of the different geometries and pendants as tools they could be likened to a hammer, which is an essential tool for building a house.

It would be almost impossible for you to build a house without a hammer and yet, when you are done you are given the credit for building the house, not the hammer. Thus, a tool helps you leverage energy, and it is empowering. Too often if a tool helps us leverage mental, emotional, or spiritual energy we get caught in the false belief that it is a "crutch," and we are a weaker person for relying on a physical tool outside of ourselves.

A crutch is a useful tool if you have a broken leg and right now all our higher connections have been compromised. Modern technology is fragmenting us. We are broken and could use the support of an alternate, balancing technology to become whole again.

The Woven Spiral Star (Fig. 9-7), like many of the tools that we have created, has evolved dramatically since it was first introduced in 1985 as a simple 6-pointed star welded out of metal with a wooden handle. We would like to go into depth with this piece so you can understand some of the reasoning that we apply to all our tools.

The 6-pointed star made of 2 overlapping triangles balances and integrates higher and lower chakras into relationship.

Fig. 9-7

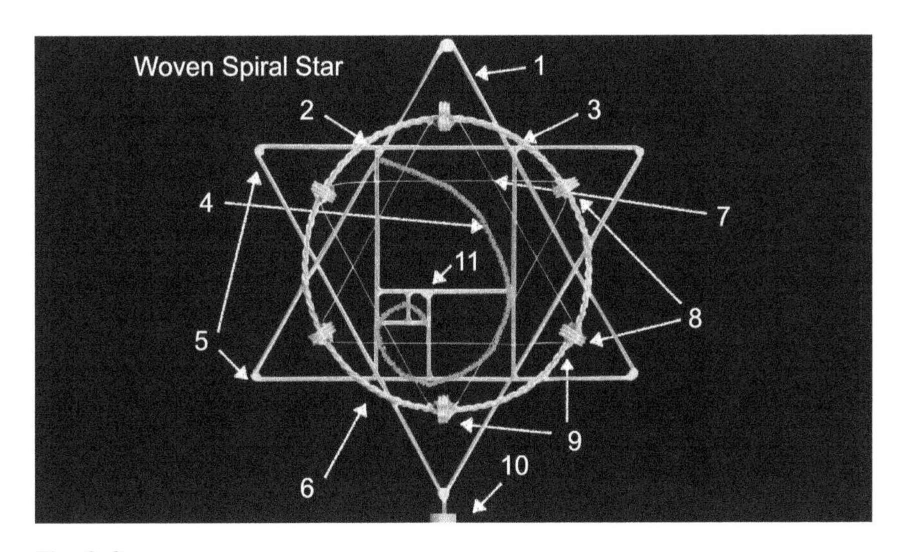

Fig. 9-8

Follow along in Fig. 9-8:

1. Each side is 9 inches long, which is a harmonic of light and the sacred measure of 18 inches used by Freemasons in the Middle Ages. The metal is silicon bronze, which is some- times referred to as "bell bronze" because it has an internal crystalized structure creating a sharper sound that increases energy flow as well. We use this metal in all our forms for its energy conductance and strength as pure copper will easily bend. Although it is 96 percent copper, the extra silicon and manganese make a big difference. We also gold-plate the forms because it increases conductivity and helps interphase with higher dimensional realms, anti-gravity, and dimensional travel.
2. Each side is woven over and then under its neighboring side
3. This sets up a spinning of the energy in a clockwise vortex.
4. Arrow points toward a spiraling image of energy created by a phi ratio rectangle reducing into smaller phi ratio rectangles with a magnet at the phi ratio balance point (11).
5. This is referencing all 7 of the magnets used at the phi point and on each tip of the 6-pointed star. The outer magnets oscillate between North and South Pole orientation. We've chosen samarium cobalt magnets because they offer the greatest bio affinity for a healthy physical response.
6. Pointing to our triple woven Causal Ring that can be used over different forms to add a powerful toroidal vortex. Here it is welded to the star. Weaving it of 3 strands allows it to access higher dimensional realms. Its length is that of a sacred Egyptian cubit.

7. This highlights a center 6-pointed star; made from pure sterling silver and woven to reinforce the spinning energy vortex.
8. There are 6 clockwise spirals of 3 turns each that act as boosters speeding up the energy flow of the Causal Ring.
9. Inside each spiral are natural hematite magnets that have been magnetized with the South pole directed toward the center forcing a stronger toroidal flow. They are cut into double 6-sided pyramids and they insulate the sterling silver star at the center, creating a stronger oscillating dynamic between the 2 woven stars.
10. Directing us toward the hardwood handle, which insulates the user's energy field from the Woven Spiral Star.

The Woven Spiral Star is a tool that balances the physical body with the healing relationship of the golden mean in unity with the 6-pointed star. When moved around your body it starts cleansing your aura. It balances energies, clears the effects of stress, and releases cellular blockages and pain to enhance chakra energy flow. This form also assists in maintaining your natural rhythm and creating a relaxed, peaceful feeling as it is moved in circles and figure eights a few inches out from the body.

It works as a filter for intent and sound. Words and sounds resonate through this form for a deep reception of the message and more profound energy healing as you place your intent through the Woven Spiral Star. A strong drum beat or vibrating tuning fork can be focused through the face or vibrationally through the metal form.

The 5G Soulution is seen hanging on its stand at the left side of Fig. 9-9. It is spinning over the Sphere of Health with a Causal Ring sitting underneath in the middle of the stand base to enhance the toroidal flow of energy in the vertical alignment of forms. Underneath, which can be separated by a table, is an additional form adding to the stacked energies. It is a Divine Co-Creator turning at a very precise speed on a special motor called the Causal Generator. This motor generates and broadcasts specific frequencies through the Causal Ring resting on its hemispherical surface. On the right side are close up images of the Sphere of Health, 5G Soulution, Divine Co-Creator, and Divine Integrator in the lower right.

The 5G Soulution (Fig. 9-9), overcomes electromagnetic and toxic chaos that blocks us from higher connection. It transforms your environment, allowing coherent energies to elevate the vibration of your body and mind to feel centered and connected.

By itself or combined with other geometries, it opens a portal of consciousness and love that is calming, centering, and healing. It has become one of the most powerful tools we have for overcoming electromagnetic chaos and environmental toxins.

The success of the 5G Soulution does not come from building a wall to protect yourself, as we discussed in Chapter 2, since the mindset regarding protection springs from fear. If a protection device were able to block EMFs, then your cell phone and all the other electronics dependent on those frequencies would stop working.

The better way is to raise the vibrational level of your field. The 5G Soulution bypasses the 3D issue by creating an influx of higher dimensional energies. When I turned the first model on, Gail remarked how our space shifted. It felt like it did several years earlier when we were without electricity for weeks because of a major flood. The peace and quiet was one of the positive experiences of that "disaster," and now with this technology we could once again experience the welcomed field of calm and connection.

The form has a steel core wrapped with copper and titanium. It is designed to spin within a woven toroidal coil with natural hematite magnets. It comes with an Advanced I.Connect that is placed under the focus of a coil with a Herkimer diamond at the end. It includes the phi ratio in its top tetrahedral pyramid and has 4320° on its surface angles to align with and be empowered by the spectrum of energy that surrounds us.

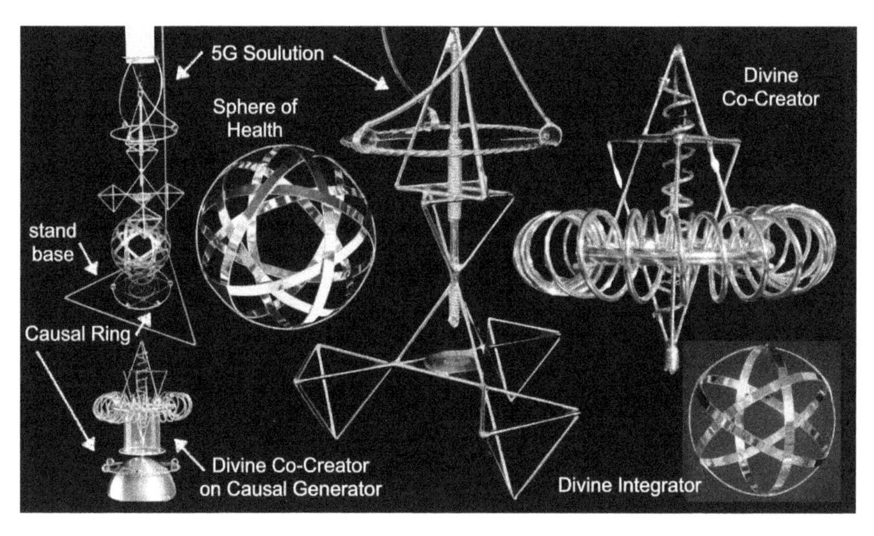

Fig. 9-9

The Causal Ring (Fig. 9-9) creates a strong, toroidal flow of energy from higher dimensions with its triple-braided gold ring, natural hematite magnets, and woven sterling silver 6-pointed star. It dramatically increases the flow of energy through the entire column of geometries and any form it is placed on.

The Sphere of Health (Fig. 9-9) has been found to support our body's innate ability to heal itself. The Sphere is designed to spin or be held near the heart or over the crown generating a peaceful and balanced environment that radiates outward and gracefully activates a natural flow of healing energy.

With intent, it will radiate Divine healing that affects us on physical, emotional, and mental levels. This energy triggers rejuvenation at a core level, making it easier to understand our lives in new ways, developing new patterns and awareness for improved health and well-being.

As seen in Fig. 9-10 the Sphere of Health resonates with several divine harmonics that have been shared earlier. It equals the number of degrees in a 20-sided icosahedron, added to a 12-sided dodecahedron, and the intertwining as duals of these 2 platonic solids always occurs in a phi ratio relationship.

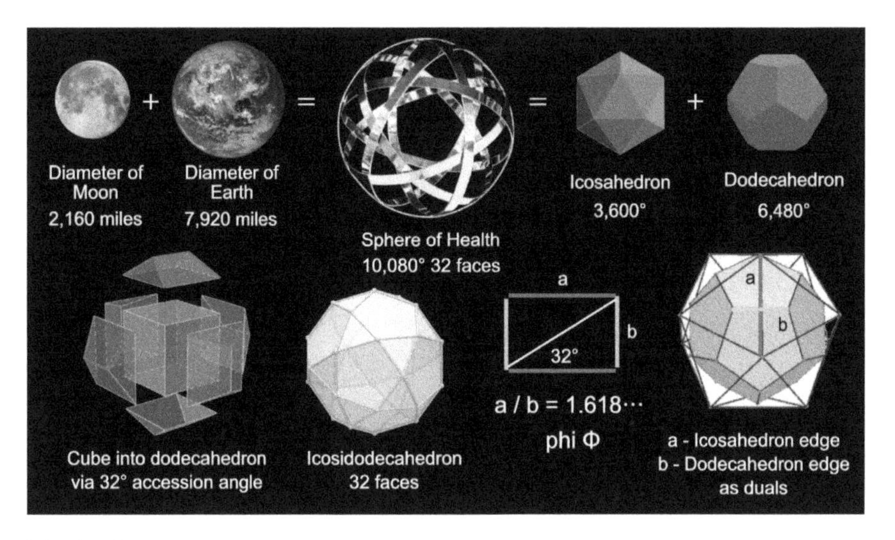

Fig. 9-10

Removing the points from the dual creates the 32 faced Icosidodecahedron and then expanding this geometry into the 6 curved bands of a sphere enhances the transformational qualities of the Divine Feminine. The diameter of the moon added to the diameter of the Earth is also equal to the 10080° of the Sphere of Health when translated from miles. The earth + moon, phi ratio, and this geometric form are harmonically resonant with each other. Its 32 faces create a harmonic with the ascension angle of 32° found in a phi ratio rectangle and the angle rising from the mundane level of earth held by the cube into the higher etheric realms revealed by the dodecahedron. (see more near Fig. 8-9)

The Divine Integrator (Fig-9-9 lower right and Fig. 5-4) works with the Universal structure of time and space, which takes you into the original source code. It cleanses, balances, and amplifies higher vibrational energy for aligning the physical body with the spiritual body, connecting you to your divine essence of love.

This form creates a toroidal flow of cleansing energy that raises the frequency of the environment. It helps facilitate deep meditation, alignment, and intuition. You can use it to manifest what has not yet materialized in your life.

Its total number of degrees (3600°) aligns it with the building blocks of creation, the 360° circle and square. The icosahedron, resonant with water and the realms of Soul, also has 3600°. Its orthogonal projections allow it to touch upon every square root of creation and as a spherical projection of a cuboctahedron it brings in the healing energies of the Divine Feminine. We include it in most of the healing spaces that we create and chose three of its projected images for the energetic face of our Heart & Soul Companion. This strongly aligns the person wearing one of these pendants with the larger geometric form being activated by a Causal Generator or 5G Soulution.

The Divine Co-Creator (Fig. 9-9) forms a phi ratio vortex raising the physical body into divine relationship, while expanding and activating the brain into a state of elevated consciousness. Rotating on the Causal Generator it fills a room with a high light vibration that touches everything and everyone in the space. Additionally, it can be placed under a table holding the 5G Soulution as it is spinning over a form, which moves you to a deep place of transformation.

The center is a Star Tetrahedron, which is resonant with the energetic shape of a photon of light. It has been expanded into a phi ratio configuration, which is aligned with life and supports a toroidal coil of 27 revolutions moving clockwise around it. The tube within the coil holds an alchemical mix of minerals and crystals charged in our activating chambers. The vertical, center spiral of 9 wraps uses 3 wires to develop a high vibrational Tesla Coil as it interacts with the outer torus. The radiating heart of the piece is a special titanium and carbon-fiber infinity, wrapped magnet.

Fig. 9-11

The Causal Generator (Fig. 9-11, spins Metatron's Cube) was created to spin our various Sacred Geometry Metaforms at a precise speed that optimizes the energy. Inside the stainless-steel hemisphere, we generate an essential frequency in the megahertz range for aligning with the higher dimensional realms.

This special frequency passes through a number of internal antenna systems and an alchemical mix of 14 essential minerals and crystals before it is directed through the cover. It radiates outward through the woven sterling silver spokes at the center of the Causal Ring. This special frequency is perfectly matched to the precise rotational speed that we carefully adjust by hand in each handmade Causal Generator.

Precise rotation of geometric forms interphases them with the rotations of time and expands their field. A rotating geometry also interacts more strongly with the biodynamics of living organisms.

Metatron's Cube (fig. 9-11, sitting on Causal Generator) is a form that is about connection, all the way to the angelic and archangelic realms for the higher good, because it is working with the principles of Creation in the physical world. With this form, you can experience unity, greater understanding, and order within your life.

It helps with grounding, so it's wonderful to be held on a point under your bed or in an environment for sleep, relaxation, and deep release of blocks for forgiveness and gratefulness. It is a strong grounding tool for manifesting your higher purpose and gaining greater focus, clarity, and gratitude.

It contains 2 interlocking tetrahedrons, an octahedron at its center, and a cube surrounding everything. These 3 platonic solids focus on the physical to anchor universal order. For good reason it is in the center of the grounding side of the pendants.

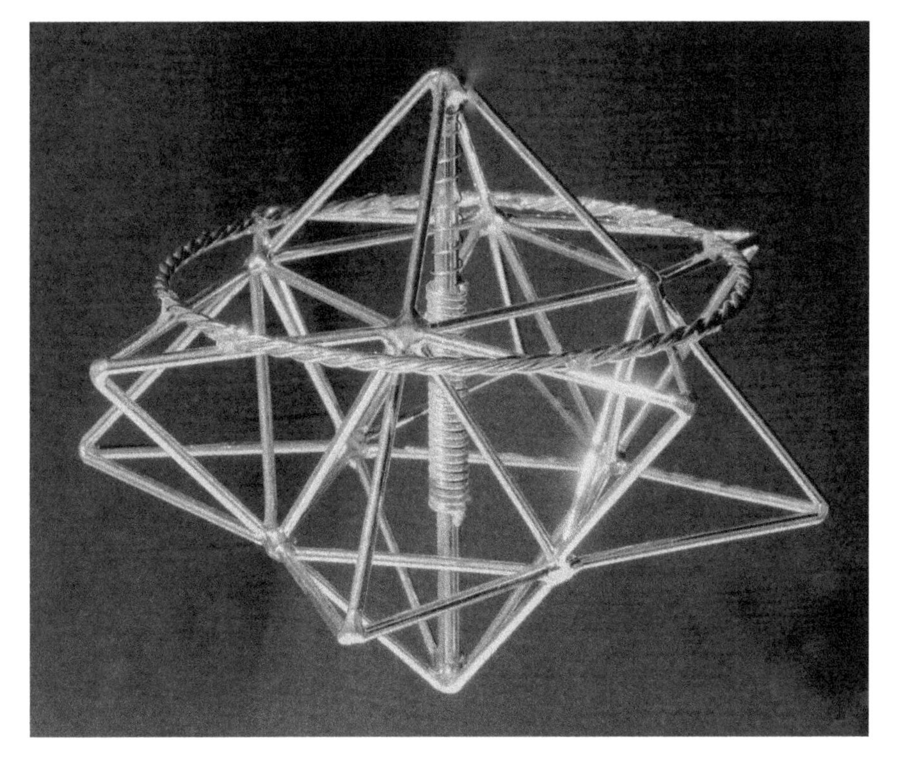

Fig. 9-12

Merkabah of Oneness (Fig. 9-12) Sit underneath the Merkabah of Oneness for a deep transcendental meditation that easily connects you to higher realms of consciousness. It generates a field of peace, harmony, oneness, and connection. This energy offers health and vitality, while creating sacred space in your environment.

It contains the same platonic solids as Metatron's Cube, but in reverse order. A twisted cube is at the center with an octahedron split in half for the top and bottom. The 8 tetrahedral tips that were inside are now radiating outward from the equator. This reversal of form expands the energies into very high dimensional realms. We added a Tesla coil, which resulted in a steel core wrapped with 27 rounds of copper and 9 rounds of titanium. A toroidal ring was placed at a right angle to create the correct transfer dynamic. Later in its development we discovered that shifting the octagonal top and bottom into Giza pyramid replicas greatly increased the energy flow and its qualities.

In the last chapter we talked about the 10,800 stanzas in the Rigveda, a 4,000-year-old Vedic scripture, and the same number being assigned to the number of bricks in the Indian fire-altar. We may never know their exact intent, but we can pull it out of mental conjecture and bring these numbers into the realm of experience.

It took a lot of work to construct the Rigveda to have exactly 10,800 stanzas and for each one to consist of 40 syllables. Multiplying one by the other gives us 432,000. These must have been very important numbers, but rather than think about them directly, let's add units of measure to them and see what they make in the physical realm of experience. If we work with the exact numbers, then 432,000 as miles equals the radius of the sun. If we examine 10,800 in miles, it becomes the sum of the moon's diameter of 2,160 miles, and the sun's diameter of

864,000 miles reduced by two magnitudes to 8,640 miles. These relationships give us the sense that the ancients were drawing on two of the most important archetypes in all our lives: the sun and the moon.

Are there universal archetypes that might be involved here? If we add degrees to these numbers and construct the geometries that represent them, then something truly magical occurs as we've been discussing all along: there are geometries that reflect these divine relationships, and they can attract and radiate an energy that can be experienced. These are energies that are aligned with the numbers that have been passed down within sacred texts for thousands of years.

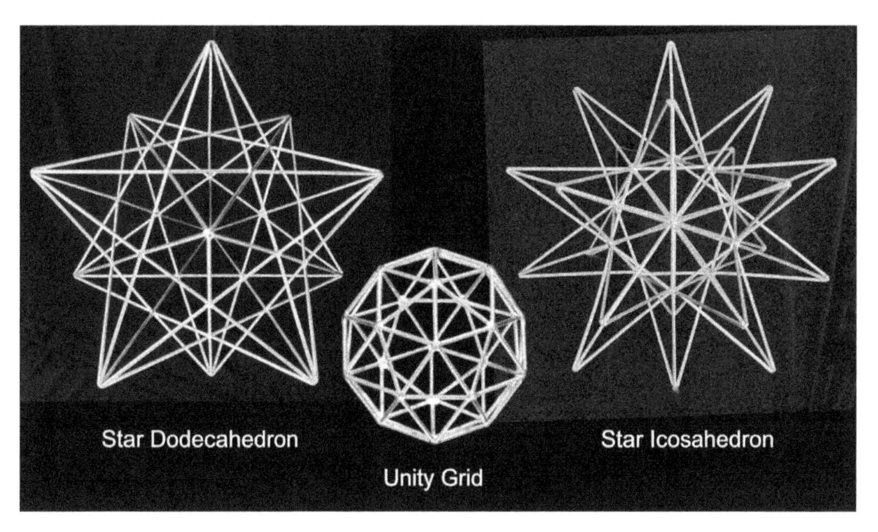

Fig. 9-13

The 3 geometries in Fig. 9-13 reflect these ancient numerical relationships. More information is shared near Fig. 8-10 in the last chapter.

Star Dodecahedron (Fig. 9-13) stimulates spiritual awakening, greater love, and compassion. It activates the heart chakra to renew deep appreciation for life with its 12 stellated points that activate balance of masculine and feminine energy.

The base length times 1.618..., phi, equals the edge length of the pyramidal points on both the dodecahedron and icosahedron. For the Star Dodecahedron this creates 12 interlocking pentagrams (5-pointed stars). If one connects the tips of the pyramids an icosahedron is formed and if the tips of the Star Icosahedron are connected, then a dodecahedron is created. Both platonic solids can dance back and forth in this manner through infinity.

Star Icosahedron (Fig. 9-13) helps you joyfully experience divine grace, love, and higher knowing. Use it to align with inner guidance to help achieve your goals, new horizons, advance creativity, and increased awareness. It works with higher levels of divine light focused on activating the pineal gland (third eye). It supports downloading higher levels of information and soul connection.

The Unity Grid (Fig. 9-13, more information near Fig. 8-12 in the last chapter) supports the different emotional, mental, and physical bodies, bringing them into relationship with the higher realms so there's a stronger sense of unity and connection. This helps in creating relationships with people, the earth, and all life. This tool is very effective in accessing information and projecting your higher intentions into the planetary grid itself, for the health and well-being of all those around you. It creates a sacred space through gratitude, respect, and appreciation.

The Unity Grid grows out of the intertwining of the icosahedron and dodecahedron as duals. To fit together the side of the icosahedron is 1.618···, phi, times the length of the dodecahedron side. The resulting shape displays the way energy flows around the planet as discovered by the Russians in the 1980s and is referred to as the Earth Grid. If we connect the points of the icosahedron to the points of the dodecahedron and remove the original structure of both forms, we are left with 30 diamond shapes whose long length (where the icosahedron side was) divided by the short distance of the diamond (where the dodecahedron side was) is equal to 1.618···, phi. To create the Unity Grid, we put the dodecahedron back into the form with 30 diamond-shaped planes, which effectively cuts each one in half, creating 60 triangles. Each triangle is equal to one of the faces of the Giza pyramid.

Fig. 9-14

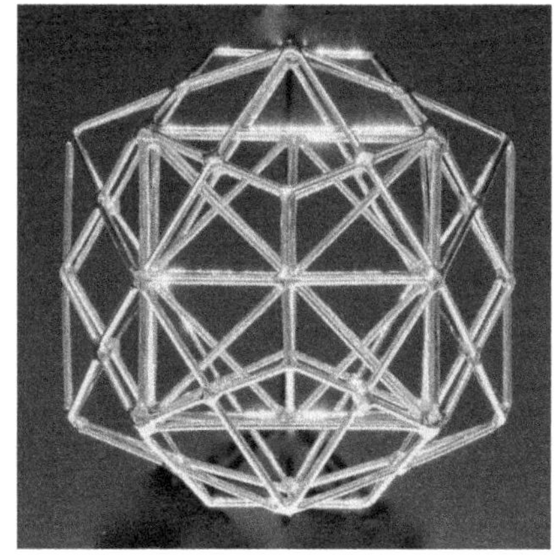

Fig. 9-15

Stellated Earth Grid (Fig. 9-14) enhances personal power, assists in creative expression and productivity as it aligns you with your purpose. It harmonizes group dynamics, creating sacred space with a large universal field. Spin it to create deep grounded inner peace that helps shift a chaotic environment into order. It aids in performing energetic work for the planet through the Earth Grid.

Its creation comes from taking the Earth Grid in Fig. 8-12 in the last chapter and placing 5-sided phi ratio pyramids on the dodecahedron that is part of its structure. Emphasizing the dodecahedron over the icosahedron is important for grounding the energy into organic matter, human beings, and activating the heart chakra, which is the doorway to higher consciousness. In a similar vein, adding the dodecahedron back into the Unity Grid also helps soften the energy and makes it more bioavailable.

Cosmic Egg (Fig. 9-15) The 5 platonic solids: tetrahedron, cube, octahedron, icosahedron, and dodecahedron combine into one beautiful and powerful Sacred Geometry. This form is perfect for supporting you in these transformative times to take a fresh look at your life and engage with a new evolutionary cycle that can clear and evolve relationships in your life.

Meditate with the Cosmic Egg to reach higher realms in a heartful and transcendent experience for raising consciousness. Working with this form stimulates deep creativity and access to manifestation.

To create the Cosmic Egg, we take Metatron's Cube containing an octahedron at the core surrounded by 2 interpenetrating tetrahedrons. Connecting the points of the tetrahedrons forms a cube and then adding the Earth Grid, which is made of the dodecahedron intertwining with the icosahedron, on the outside of the cube completes the set of five platonic solids.

This is a fractal progression of light starting with a photon (Star Tetrahedron) as the seed. 32°, the angle of ascension lifts the side of the dodecahedron off the face of the cube (Earth) to incorporate the higher vibrational aspects of the icosahedron and dodecahedron.

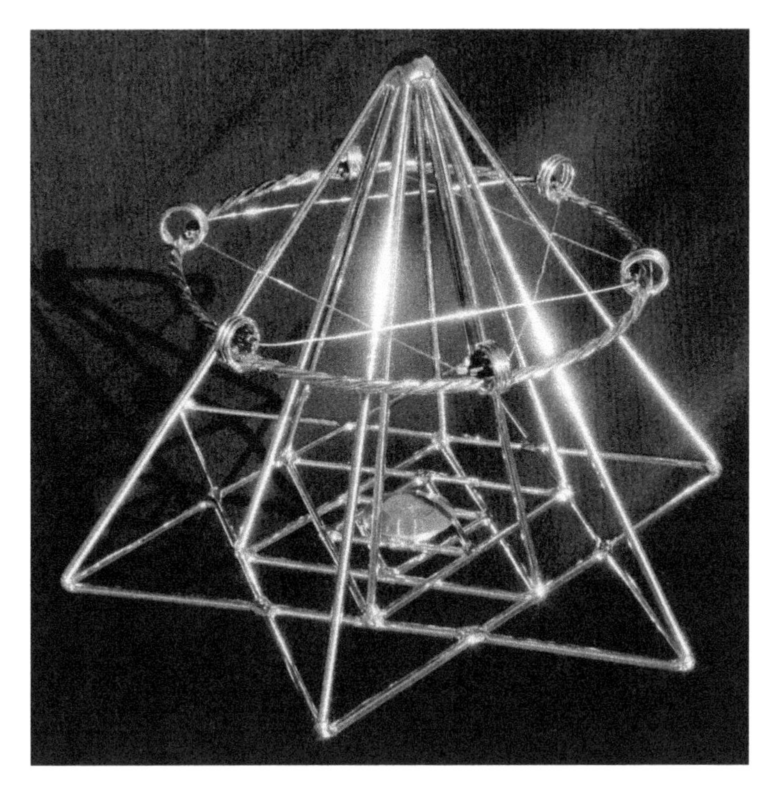

Fig. 9-16

Aquarian Pyramid (Fig. 9-16) establishes a direct link to Source to better understand your purpose, inner guidance, past lives, and manifestation. It helps align meridians and chakras to higher frequencies and grounds these energies into the body. Use it to raise the energy of crystals, water, and substances placed within or nearby.

This is the evolution of the first form Gregory created in 1982 after attending a workshop with Dr. Frank Alper. Dr. Alper suggested bringing the 6-pointed star into 3D resonance by placing a tetrahedron over each triangular tip. Gregory extended the outside edge of each tetrahedron upward to meet with the other extended sides, forming a 6-sided pyramid. We still make the connectors to build this form as a large pyramid that people can sit and meditate in. The newest version has three 6-pointed stars radiating out from the center with edges rising from both the outside tips and those of the next inner star. The difference in length is the $\sqrt{3}$, which creates a very active dynamic within this pyramid. With the Causal Ring placed over the point a toroidal vortex of continually cleansing energy is created, powerful enough to clear a room or a home. The center cup has a hole in its center to allow the toroidal energy vortex to pass through while adding the energies of whatever is placed within: gems, flower essences, homeopathies, or an Advanced I.Connect for a healing set up that could be placed under the 5G Soulution or on a Causal Generator.

HANDHELD WELLNESS TOOLS

Some of our Sacred Geometry tools (Woven Spiral Star Fig. 9-7 & Dorji, Fig. 9-17) can be held in hand and moved over a person to open and shift energy through their different chakras where the tool is placed or rotated in circles, figure eights and broad sweeping movements. These tools allow you to target a particular area of your body or a specific chakra to help clear blocks and issues.

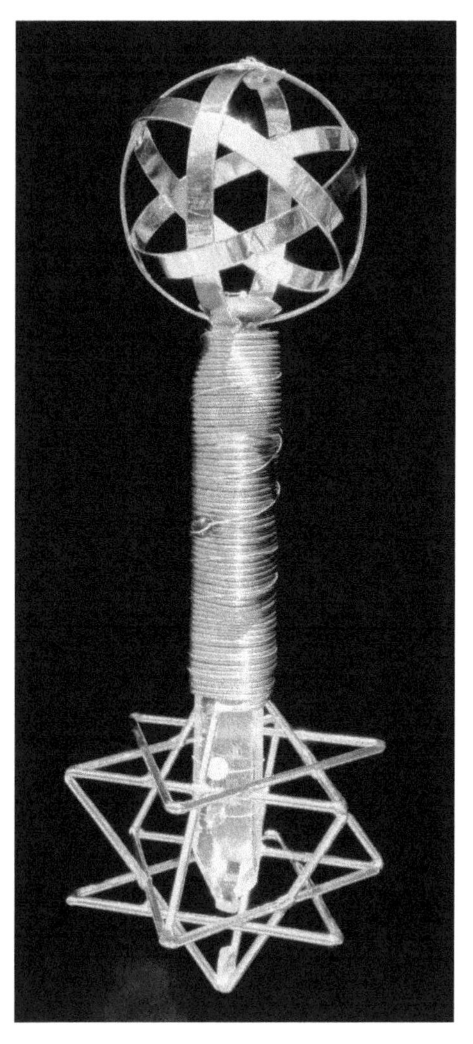

Fig. 9-17

Dorji of Divine Integration (Fig. 9-17) is a tool for working on yourself and others to absorb, release, and redirect energy flows. It's one of the most powerful healing tools that we have for moving and integrating life's positive energy flows. By moving the Dorji over the body or placing it where needed, it can release toxins and emotions, open flows of energy within and between your chakras, clear past life issues fostering generational healing, and stimulate the third eye and crown for greater spiritual awakening. Energy flows in through the spherical end and out through the point. While lying down, place the Dorji on the body between chakras to integrate their energies or between the legs with the point away from the body for a profound grounding into Mother Earth. It may also be placed above the head with the point directed away from the body for a higher dimensional connection.

An eight-and-a-half-inch lab-grown crystal is activated in our chambers and becomes the centerpiece of our gold-plated 14-inch tool. A spherical Divine Integrator on one end balances the 5D Star Tetrahedron on the opposite end. Within the Divine Integrator on the end is a simplified I.Connect. Copper and sterling silver coiled around the crystal move energy from one end to the other activating 9 added jewels, from amethyst to a Herkimer diamond. Hidden within the copper coil are orgonite wrappings, gem mixtures, and titanium-wrapped magnets.

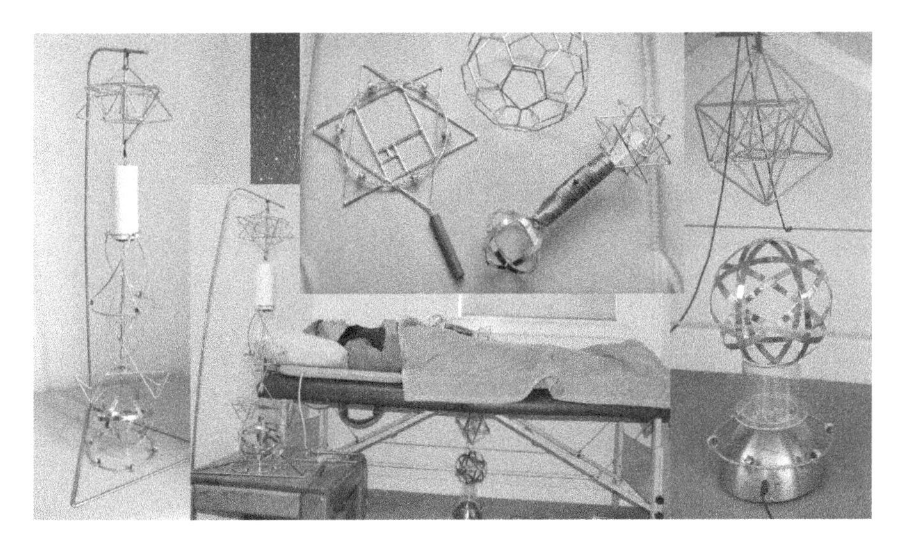

Fig. 9-18

Like gears in a machine all these forms can be exchanged and paired differently, and when a new one is added they all shift around energetically to accommodate the whole. Each person may discover a new application or use for how it works. You are the unique pivot point that Universe orbits around.

In Fig. 9-18 is one of the setups we use for our healing room. We always like the 5G Soulution on the left to be near the client. There are some healers who have three 5Gs triangulated in their meditation, or a healing room with each 5G spinning over a different form. Additional forms can be above or below in a vertical alignment to activate larger vortexes of energy.

In some cases, we put a Merkabah of Oneness above the 5G or the client for the higher access it provides. Recently we've discovered that putting a Divine Co-Creator (Fig. 9-9), spinning on a Causal Generator, in line with the 5G under the table where it is positioned creates a very deep healing space. The Dorji of Divine Integration and Woven Spiral Star can be moved over them. We usually like the spherical forms like the Divine Integrator, Sphere of Health, or Unity Grid under the 5G. In this set up we've added Metatron's Cube directly under the table to help with grounding and release. At other times we've added the Aquarian Pyramid with a Causal Ring to the room to keep the energy clear during the sessions. These are all great tools to use with your chosen healing modalities and intuition.

TAKE A MOMENT TO REFLECT . . .

Ending this chapter with the various tools found in our "healing room" begs a profound question: what is being healed? Everything shared in this book reflects the remarkable interconnectedness of Universe and our individual abilities, which are also remarkable, to break and block these same interconnections for ourselves. In addition, we've shown how modern technology has added many impediments to our connection and overcoming these difficulties is another part of the healing.

The Sacred Geometry tools we've been discussing have the ability, through harmonic resonance, to help us rediscover and rebuild our Universal connections. This is the ultimate healing that all the work done with these tools is moving us toward. Along this path moving into the higher dimensional aspects of our being, we must heal the most pressing issues first, which is often breakdown in our physical body.

Balancing the emotional body and eliminating stress on the mental level can follow soon after if we consistently work on ourselves and understand the importance of healing these higher levels of our being. When we're successful with these levels it prevents many physical diseases from developing, as science has pointed out with the negative effects of fear-based emotions and the number of diseases triggered by stress.

However, moving beyond these levels takes us into more inclusive levels of consciousness that offer healing on karmic, soul, and generational levels. These levels of healing offer a platform to be of service to all and planetary healing as a reflection of humanity's next step in spiritual evolution, which is a healing of the illusion of separation. *To be healed is to be made whole.* All of this requires inputs of energy resonant with the highest values of creation: **Universal archetypes are the blueprints for Divine alignment.**

Link to our website for more information or go directly to https://iconnect2all.com/book. To contact us via email: office@iconnect2all.com

EPILOGUE

A few weeks from the completion of writing this book (an ongoing journey for a good number of years), something quite unimaginable happened. I had a severe fall that landed me in the intensive care unit with spinal cord compression and cervical disc injury. I underwent spinal surgery a few days after the accident and am currently engaged in the epic recovery process to heal my neck and regain full feeling, mobility, and strength in my limbs.

While I was falling, I recognized it as a significant spiritual healing event that was on my karmic path. Even though I wouldn't have consciously chosen this timing or situation, I saw that it was the perfect intersection for my life. I was offered an enormous gift and am now in the process of unpacking the highs, lows, and depths of what that means.

During the fall and thereafter, my consciousness was crystal clear and rather than feeling fear, I felt peaceful and deeply connected. I was in an embrace of higher knowing that carried me through and kept my soul in the lead. I was wheeled into the operating room in the company of guides and masters as I meditated and chanted while the anesthesia took over my body. Being in that state was the catalyst for being fully present and allowing the people and events that would support my healing to come forward. My lifelong issue of asking for what

I wanted was squarely confronting me, and my vulnerability has rewarded both Gregory and me with deepening the love we have with each other. I've allowed family and friends to help me along this path in ways I have formally resisted—a real blow to my ego and persona of being a strong woman. It's rough not being in control!

During intense periods of physical and emotional pain, I disliked the effects of drugs and listened to my body calling for love, not numbness. It was the focus on love that helped the pain fall away. When I feel frustrated at the length of this healing process, I remind myself that the turtle's journey is a noble one that moves me out of my habit of pushing and into allowing. I've learned to be more patient as I struggle with the reality of wearing a neck brace 24/7 for 12 weeks and relying on Gregory for so many simple things.

We have been working with these universal principles and archetypes for over 40 years. We've meditated daily with the geometries you've seen in this book and have always been diligent with our practice. The care of mind, body, and soul is a lifelong path that offers us the perfect transformation that is Spirit's calling. Early in the year I was told that this is the year of greater receiving than what I'd known. It's always humorous how the mind likes to interpret these edicts and paint a picture that can be quite different from what is unveiled. Yet, I am humbled to experience the abundant love, compassion, and generosity that I'm receiving, which heals my soul throughout so many lifetimes. These are the things that are immeasurable and have spiraling impact.

Epilogue

We come into this life and experience the transition from unity, wholeness, and full connection. We must learn to navigate an individual body in a dense physical dimension that can build the muscles of connection and love. Distractions, separation, and pain are the doorways we wander through to find our way back home. All along, the Universal principles and archetypes of creation have been staring us in the face, calling to us to remember who we are truly meant to be. They remain within our reach to open to the love of consciousness that is our origin and salvation.

The archetypes of creation are meant to be integrated into our physical lives so we might live a multidimensional life that is abundant with love, gratitude, and compassion. What an amazing journey we are on. Enjoy the ride.

With abundant love and blessings, Gail

ABOUT THE AUTHORS

Link to our website for more information or go directly to https://iconnect2all.com/book. To contact us via email: office@ iconnect2all.com